ENGLAND AND INDIA

ENGLAND AND INDIA

A RECORD OF PROGRESS DURING

A HUNDRED YEARS

1785-1885

ROMESH C. DUTT, I.C.S., C.I.E.

GYAN

Published by

Gyan Publishing House
5, Ansari Road
Daryaganj, New Delhi-110002
Phone: 011-47034999, 9811692060
E-mail: books@gyanbooks.com

Distribution Network
gyanbooks.com
India, USA, Canada, UK, Australia, France

ISBN: 978-81-212-9318-1 (PB)
First Published,1897

2nd Impression 2023

Printed at: Gyan Press, Delhi.

ENGLAND AND INDIA

Author: ROMESH C. DUTT

ENGLAND AND INDIA

ENGLAND AND INDIA

A RECORD OF PROGRESS DURING A HUNDRED YEARS

1785—1885

BY

ROMESH C. DUTT, I.C.S., C.I.E.

LATE OFFICIATING COMMISSIONER OF ORISSA, AND SUPERINTENDENT OF ORISSA TRIBUTARY STATES IN INDIA

SOMETIME MEMBER OF THE LEGISLATIVE COUNCIL OF THE LIEUTENANT-GOVERNOR OF BENGAL

AUTHOR OF 'CIVILIZATION IN ANCIENT INDIA,' ETC.

LONDON

CHATTO & WINDUS

1897

CONTENTS

PREFACE

The present year has been a year of rejoicing all over the British Empire in all parts of the globe; in India it has been the most disastrous year since the country passed under British rule. A severe plague has all but depopulated the great cities of one province; a destructive earthquake has ruined the towns and villages of another; and a famine, the most widespread in its area ever known in India, has desolated the country from one extremity to the other.

But the famine of 1897 is only one of a series of such calamities which have visited India almost periodically within the present century. Famines are a thing of the past in Western Europe; in India every generation, every period of twenty years, has its tale of distress to tell. The year of the accession of the Queen was marked by a severe famine which desolated Northern India, and counted its victims by the million. The year of the Indian Mutiny was the commencement of the next twenty years, marked by three great famines—the famines of the North-West, of Orissa, and of Behar. The year in which the Queen assumed the title of the Empress of India was the year of a more terrible famine in Madras, which swept away five millions of the people of Southern India. And the year of the Queen's Diamond Jubilee has, unfortunately, been marked in India by another widespread famine which embraces the greater part of India within its sphere, and which, in spite of relief operations, is likely to count its victims by the million. The years 1837, 1857, 1877, and 1897 are sad landmarks in the modern history of India—landmarks not of progress and prosperity, but of desolation and disasters.

Englishmen will not contemplate these facts with complaisance. It is not gratifying to know that a country, possessing a rich and fertile soil, and a frugal and industrious population, is still subject to recurring famines after a century and a half of British rule. It is not pleasant to learn that, after an uninterrupted peace of forty years, the people of India show no signs of increasing prosperity and greater security from distress. And it is sad to contemplate that, in spite of a civilized administration, of the construction of railways and canals, of the vast extension of cultivation, and of the prosperity of foreign trade, India is still periodically desolated by calamities such as are unknown in Europe.

The great famine in Bengal of 1770 aroused the attention of Englishmen to the defects of the East India Company's administration in the last century, and was followed by the Regulating Act in 1774, by Pitt's India Act in 1784, and by Lord Cornwallis's Permanent Settlement of Bengal in 1793. Unless we are greatly mistaken, the sad events of the present year will once more direct the attention of Englishmen to Indian affairs, and will lead to reforms which are urgently needed. Under the Company's rule, the renewal of the Charter every twenty years was an occasion for an inquiry into Indian affairs. We have lost the salutary effect of those periodical inquiries now, and the direct administration of India by the Crown has, along with many great and obvious advantages, this one disadvantage—that the administration is virtually responsible to none. But although the periodical inquiries into Indian administration have unfortunately been discontinued, recent events are directing the attention of Englishmen to Indian affairs, and will before long require some investigation into the condition of the Indian people. Thoughtful men will ask themselves if the recurrence of destructive famines, five times within the forty years of the direct government of India by the Crown, indicates the normal state of a rich and fertile country; and if the death of eight or ten millions of human beings from starvation, within this period, indicates the normal condition of an industrial and frugal population living in uninterrupted peace. These are questions which will require some definite inquiry and some definite answer.

And if an impartial inquiry be made into these matters, as it must sooner or later, it will be found that the present administration of India, honest and able as it undoubtedly is, has drifted into some serious blunders. And the worst of these blunders is its inordinate expenditure, which is impoverishing the people, and making them defenceless against droughts and famines. It will be found that the continuous increase of the State-demand from the produce of the soil, which is virtually the only means of subsistence for the mass of the people in India, is making them incapable of saving in good years, and resourceless in bad years. It will be found that the imperial policy of England in the east, to secure a 'scientific frontier,' and to maintain an adequate army against Russia at the cost of India, is exhausting that rich and fertile country. It will be found that a system of almost unlimited borrowing of English capital, and of increasing the public debt of

India in times of peace, drains the resources of the country for the payment of the interest in gold. And it will be found that the non-representation of the views and opinions of the people in the administration of the country makes it weak and uninformed in essential matters, wanting in touch with the people, and ignorant of the real condition and even the real poverty of the voiceless millions.

'It is an inherent condition of human affairs,' says John Stuart Mill in his work on 'Representative Government,' 'that no intention, however sincere, of protecting the interests of others, can make it safe or salutary to tie up their own hands.' And the events of the last forty years prove that it is necessary, in order to protect the vital interests of the people of India, to give them some voice in the administration of their own affairs, and to concede to them some form of representation such as it is safe and wise and practicable to concede in India. Different classes of British manufacturers and merchants, capitalists and planters, have the means to press their demands on the Indian Government for the remission of particular duties, or the construction of new lines of railway, for the maintenance of special labour laws, or for accelerating or retarding reforms in civil or criminal laws; and the Government of India has, not unoften, shaped its acts in furtherance of the interests of such classes. The people of India have no such means to press their demands even for necessary and reasonable reforms; they have no constitutional methods for expressing their wishes or explaining their views; and their interests are not adequately protected, because they are not constitutionally represented. Instances in which the interests of the people have suffered in the past, because not duly represented, can be cited without number; nor is it possible to adequately safeguard their interests in the future unless they be represented in some manner in the Government of their country. 'By their own hands only,' continues Mill, 'can any positive and durable improvement of their circumstances in life be worked out;' and the time is near when Englishmen will see it fit and desirable to allow to the people of India some voice and some power, duly guarded, in improving their circumstances in life.

A brief retrospect of the past history of India on such an occasion as this may enable us to understand Indian problems, and may help the cause of reform; for the history of British rule in India has been a history of reforms in the past, and justifies the hope for reforms in the future. The forlorn pessimism which recognises no progress in Indian administration in the past is both foolish and false; while the conventional optimism which shrinks from any reforms in Indian administration in the future is equally silly and hurtful. The problems before us at the present moment are momentous and serious, and, in order to face those problems with an unbiased mind, we must honestly and gratefully recognise the progress which has been effected in the past, and earnestly and hopefully strive after needed reforms in the future. As an Indian who has carefully studied the history of his country during the present century, who has witnessed the great events which have taken place in India during the last forty years, and who has taken his humble share in the work of Indian administration during a quarter of a century, the writer of these pages has honestly endeavoured to place the real needs of his country and the views of his countrymen before the British public.

It is scarcely necessary to add that the present little work is not meant to be a review of the general history of India, but is rather a review of reforms and popular progress in India in the past, and a forecast of the reforms needed in the future. I have not attempted to narrate in detail the story of wars and conquests, of military triumphs and annexations. The triumphs of peace effected by such rulers as Cornwallis and Bentinck, Munro and Elphinstone, Canning and Ripon, are more relevant to my purpose, and have been narrated more fully, because they have an abiding influence in benefiting and elevating my countrymen. And behind the work of these great and gifted rulers of India, I note the influence of those great English statesmen at home who have led great movements towards reform and progress in England, who have inspired reforms and progress in India, and who have given their names to the ages in which they lived. I have referred again and again to their work and to English history, because the history of progress in England and the history of progress in India have flowed in parallel streams. Indian history, or rather the history of Indian progress under British rule, is unintelligible without a reference to the history of progress in England.

Such a clear understanding of the causes of progress in the past inspires us with hope for progress in the future. And in the midst of the calamities which have overtaken India in the present year, and amidst the difficulties which surround Indian administration in the future, there is the solacing fact that the times are in our favour, that reforms in England must lead to reforms in India, and that India forms a part of that great modern empire which has accepted progress and self-government as its dominating ideas.

ROMESH C. DUTT.

SANDGATE,
August, 1897.

ENGLAND AND INDIA

CHAPTER I.

THE AGE OF PITT AND WELLINGTON.

1785—1815.

THE recent celebration of the Queen's Diamond Jubilee naturally recalls to mind the memorable events, within and beyond the limits of the United Kingdom, which have led to the consolidation of the British Empire during the present century. Our attention is called to those bold enterprises, and to that policy of wisdom, which have helped to draw closer various nations, living in different latitudes and under different skies, who agree, however, in rendering a common homage to the Queen of England. And along with the story of the extension and consolidation of the British Empire, the still more instructive story of social, moral, and intellectual progress, and of the advancement of the people in influence and power, is vividly brought to our mind by the great festival of the present year, a festival unique in the history of England, a festival of the completion of a sixty years' reign.

Such an occasion seems to be appropriate for placing before the British public a brief record of the progress which India has made under British rule. The story of the rise of the Indian Empire has been told in voluminous works, as well as in short and entertaining books, and it is not with the purpose of repeating a twice-told tale that this little work has been undertaken. Our main object in the present narration will be to tell the story of progress, and trace the steady advancement of the people. The current of popular progress is often obscured in history by the shadow of larger events; but, nevertheless, this obscure stream spreads over and vivifies the land from age to age, and is worth more to the people than the most glorious wars and brilliant victories which historians love to narrate.

It is needless to remind our readers that, in tracing the history of progress in India, it will be our duty to frequently refer to extraneous causes—to those great impulses which are making for progress in England and in Europe. These causes are not always explained by the historians of India with sufficient distinctness. Filled with a legitimate admiration for the great actors on the scene, the historians of India often forget that those actors receive their cue from Europe, and that their most memorable acts are determined by great European movements. We have heard it said by responsible statesmen in India that the destinies of that country should never be brought under the varying influences of English politics. That there should be a certain consistency in the policy of the Indian Government is a proposition which needs to be stated to receive universal assent. But that India should move in an orbit entirely her own, and beyond the influence of the great movements of modern Europe, is neither possible nor desirable.

To us the modern history of India is unintelligible without a reference to the modern history of England. We are unable to grasp the policy of Lord Wellesley in India without comprehending the policy of Pitt in Europe. We fail to follow the great reforms inaugurated in India by Munro, Elphinstone, and Bentinck, without knowing something of the parallel reforms effected in England at the same period by men like Cobbett and Brougham, Canning and Grey. The vigorous policy of Dalhousie receives its true explanation from the foreign policy of Palmerston; and the Liberal measures of Ripon are unintelligible without a reference to the Liberal measures of Gladstone. Throughout this century the rulers of India, whether under the East India Company or under the Crown, have drawn their inspiration from England, and the great movements which mark the history of modern England have left their impress on the history of modern India. In trying to elucidate the history of India, therefore, we shall frequently have to turn for light and guidance to episodes in English history, which are sufficiently familiar to Englishmen, but whose far-reaching results are little suspected.

The story of the rise of British power in India virtually begins from 1745. But we pass by the events of the first forty years, the events of the age of Clive and Hastings, because they have been made familiar to the English reader by that most charming of historical painters, Lord Macaulay. And the subject is worthy of his matchless pencil. There is no period of English history, probably, which is lighted by such brilliant tints or shaded by such dark shadows as this first period of British conquests in India. The strange incidents which led to the transfer of the supreme power in India from the grasp of the Great Mogul to a company of traders from the West, hitherto little known in Asia, have in them all the romance which lightens the adventures of the most daring adventurers in unknown seas and lands, like Columbus or Gama, Cortez or Pizarro. As an Anglo-Indian poet sings:

> 'History never told
> Of monarch-merchants, heroes wandering far,
> A stranger tale of traffic or of war!'

On the other hand, this strange tale of traffic and of war is disfigured by incidents which throw sombre shadows over the scene it depicts. Englishmen in the last century heard of the tale with concern, and became anxious for their good name abroad, and this feeling found eloquent expression in that most august of proceedings which even the British Parliament has ever witnessed, the impeachment of Warren Hastings.

To the end of his life, Edmund Burke felt that he had failed in the mightiest endeavour which he had made in the cause of justice and of right. But, nevertheless, if ever any man succeeded in vindicating right and justice, that man was Edmund Burke. As one of the greatest of living writers in England has pointed out, 'the side that is defeated on a particular issue is often victorious in the wide and general outcome. Looking back across the ninety years that divide us from that memorable scene in Westminster Hall, we may see that Burke had more success than at first appeared. If he did not convict the man, he overthrew a system, and stamped its principles with lasting censure and shame. . . . That Hastings was acquitted was immaterial. The lesson of his impeachment had been taught with sufficiently impressive force—the great lesson that Asiatics have rights, and that Europeans have obligations; that a superior race is bound to observe the highest current morality of the time in all its dealings with the subject race. Burke is entitled to our lasting reverence as the first apostle and great upholder of integrity, mercy, and honour, in the relation between his countrymen and their humble dependents.'*

Warren Hastings left India in 1785, and our present story begins from this date. The great Pitt had taken

* 'Burke,' by John Morley.

charge of his duties as Prime Minister of England in the preceding year, and held that high post continuously for seventeen years; and the policy of the rulers of India during these years was a reflection of the policy of Pitt in Europe. In the very first year of his tenure of office Pitt passed his famous India Bill of 1784, which placed the civil and military transactions of the East India Company under a Board of Control in England; and the British Government thus became directly responsible for the proper administration of Indian affairs. The period of Clive and Hastings came to a natural end.

Lord Rosebery has, in his Life of Pitt, dispelled a widespread misapprehension, and has shown that Pitt, who is generally regarded as a great war Minister, was really the greatest peace Minister that ever held office in England. His soul was bent on securing, not the triumphs of war, but the triumphs of peace. Three times he brought forward his scheme of Parliamentary Reform—the last time in 1785; but England was not yet ripe for it, and in spite of the zeal and ability of Pitt, his endeavours failed. In the same year he brought forward his generous and statesmanlike Irish scheme, proposing to admit Ireland to a participation of the commercial advantages of Great Britain, and denouncing in the strongest terms the past treatment of Ireland by England. But on this question also English prejudices prevailed; and one of the first and best opportunities for really uniting the two countries passed away. In 1787 a small colonizing expedition was sent to Australia, and the foundation was laid on which has been built up in these hundred years the great self-governing Australian colonies of the present day. In the following year Pitt, prompted by Wilberforce and supported by Burke and Fox, induced the House of Commons to take the burning question of the slave trade into consideration, and the Bill for its provisional regulation was passed shortly after. And in 1792 Pitt made his great speech on this great subject, which all authorities consider the highest effort even of his genius. He was so weak and exhausted that he took some medicine before he began to speak; but when he once began, his long and powerful oration showed no signs of weakness, and during the last twenty minutes he seemed nothing less than inspired. His great rivals on the opposite side were carried away by his eloquence; Fox and Wyndham were loud in their admiration; Sheridan was passionate in his praise, and Grey was equally enthusiastic. Such were the noble reforms which Pitt endeavoured to secure during the first nine years of his administration, from 1784 to 1793; and these years witnessed the first great reforms in the government of India.

Lord Cornwallis, the successor of Warren Hastings, landed in Calcutta in 1786. The appointment of this nobleman of high character as Governor-General of India was in itself a sign of the times; and Cornwallis did not belie expectations. The Company's servants had from the very commencement found the task of civil administration in India more difficult than the task of defeating ill-disciplined Indian armies in the field. Lord Clive, the victor of Plassy and the conqueror of Bengal, had signally failed in his system of civil administration. Under his system the administration of law and justice, as well as the collection of revenue, was still left in the hands of the Nawab of Bengal and the two deputy Nawabs of Patna and Murshidabad; and the revenue when collected was supposed to be made over to the Company. In the meantime the Company's servants were busy with the Company's trade, and also with making colossal private fortunes, with which they hoped to retire to England, as fast as possible. Thus, the supreme power, which was responsible for the well-being and protection of the people, did not concern itself with the administration of the country; while the Nawab and the deputy Nawabs and their subordinates, who were entrusted with the entire administration, did not feel that responsibility for the good of the people which the supreme power alone can feel. They were collecting revenue for the Company, and were not scrupulous as to the means employed; and the Company, so long as it obtained the revenue, believed itself free from the responsibilities of administration. Thus, under a dual system of government neither party felt responsible for good administration, and the people were grievously oppressed. The English, as the supreme power in the land, naturally got the odium for this state of things; and the thoughtful writer of the 'Siyar-ul-Mutakherin' lamented that 'the new rulers paid no attention to the concerns of the people of Hindustan, and suffered them to be mercilessly plundered, oppressed and tormented by officers of their own appointing.'

Warren Hastings totally upset the system of Lord Clive. He arrested the deputy Nawabs, and brought them down to Calcutta. A judicial inquiry was made into their conduct and administration, and their authority was abolished for ever. He removed the central revenue offices from Murshidabad and Patna to Calcutta, and placed them under the supervision of English officials under the name of the Board of Revenue. He abolished the judicial powers of local landlords or zemindars, and appointed an English officer in each district under the misleading name of Collector for the purposes of administration. The Collector was responsible for the collection of revenues; he was the Civil Judge; and he was also the Criminal Court in his district. A code of regulations was drawn up for the guidance of Collectors; and two Sadar Courts of Appeal were established at Calcutta.

These measures give evidence of Warren Hastings's energy, vigour, and power of organization; but they also give evidence of his arbitrary exercise of power. He swept away by a stroke of his pen the system which had prevailed before; he took away from local chiefs and zemindars the power and the responsibility of keeping peace within their vast territories; he rejected all co-operation on the part of the people in the administration of their own concerns; and he set up young Englishmen, ignorant of the law and the customs of the country, to administer civil and criminal justice, to collect revenues, to repress crime, to maintain peace, and to be sole authority in all matters of administration in their districts. The system could not succeed, and did not succeed.

When Lord Cornwallis came to India, his great endeavour was to make these young district Collectors upright and honest administrators. The Collectors used to draw salaries varying according to their work, and in no case exceeding about £1,500 a year; but their irregular and additional gains amounted to a great deal more. The pagoda tree was shaken to some effect in every district by the very men appointed as the heads of districts. Lord Cornwallis abolished these irregular gains of the district Collectors; and he forced the Court of Directors to grant them adequate salaries. He also effected a great improvement in the administration, which has unfortunately been lost to us since, by separating the revenue and executive work from the judicial work. He limited the powers of Collectors to revenue work only; and he appointed magistrates and judges in all districts for the performance of judicial work. And Lord Cornwallis also established four Provincial Appellate Courts, in Calcutta, Dacca, Murshidabad and Patna, between the District Courts and the Sadar Appellate Courts established by Hastings. All these measures bear the impress of Cornwallis's judicious mind, his noble English instincts, and his desire to rule India on those principles of equity and justice which are recognised in all civilized countries, rather than by despotic power. In the words of a writer, who writes with an intimate knowledge of his subject, 'The Cornwallis Code, whether for revenue, police, criminal and civil justice, or other functions, defined and set bounds to authority, created procedure, by a regular system of appeal guarded against the miscarriage of justice, and founded the Civil Service of India as it exists to this day.' In one respect only Cornwallis failed to rectify the mistakes of his predecessor: the almost entire exclusion of the people of India from the administration of their country was continued. The result proved disastrous in the end.

We pass by the story of Cornwallis's Mysore war, an account of which will be found in every book on Indian history. Tipu Sultan was humbled, and ceded one half of his territories, which were divided among the English and their allies. He also consented to pay three millions towards the expenses of the war, and sent his two sons as hostages for the fulfilment of the terms. The peace was concluded in 1792.

But the crowning glory of Lord Cornwallis's administration was the Permanent Settlement of the land revenues of Bengal, effected in 1793. The condition of the landed classes in Bengal—both landlords and cultivators

—had been reduced to the last stage of misery through the blunders as well as the rapacity of the Company's servants and their Indian subordinates. The great famine of 1771 had desolated Bengal, and had carried away a third of the population of that fertile and populous province. Cultivated fields had relapsed into jungle, and villages had become the home of the wild beast. The vigorous administration of Warren Hastings gave the country some security and rest; but his frequent and punctual calls for revenue, and his system of settling estates with the highest bidders, ruined the old landed houses of Bengal. Estates were sold to speculators; and money-lenders acquired vast properties, and screwed up rents in order to pay the demands of the Government. The result was disastrous. 'I may safely assert,' wrote Lord Cornwallis, 'that one-third of the Company's territory in Hindostan is now a jungle, inhabited only by wild beasts.'

The proposal was then made to settle the estates at a revenue fixed for ten years. The inadequacy of such a measure was, however, apparent to the Governor-General. 'Will a ten years' lease induce any proprietor to clear away that jungle, and encourage the ryots to come and cultivate his lands, when at the end of that lease he must either submit to be taxed, *ad libitum*, for his newly-acquired lands, or lose all hopes of deriving any benefits for his labour?' Lord Cornwallis therefore desired the settlement to be permanent, and the settlement was made permanent in 1793.

Those who judge the policy of Indian rulers merely by the amount of revenue which it produces have condemned this act of Lord Cornwallis. Those, however, who judge it by happiness which it secures to the people of India will admit that no single measure of the British Government that can be named has been so beneficial to the people, and therefore to the Government under which they live. Cultivation has largely extended in Bengal within these hundred years, mainly owing to the Permanent Settlement, and the profits from this extension have remained with the people, and have bettered their condition. And as the Government asks for no increase of revenue from the landlords of Bengal, they have stopped the landlords from obtaining increase from cultivators, except on the most reasonable grounds. Bengal cultivators to-day are therefore more prosperous and self-relying, more free from the grasp of the money-lender, and better able to withstand the first onset of famines than cultivators elsewhere in India. For all this—for the increased happiness which has been secured to over 50,000,000 of people in India—the credit is due to the large-hearted policy and the benevolent wisdom of Lord Cornwallis.

Among the direct benefits which the British Government have derived from the Permanent Settlement of Bengal, there are two of a specially marked character which require to be mentioned. It is not easy, says a writer whom we have already quoted, to over-estimate the advantage of having a wealthy, influential, and privileged class who have everything to lose and nothing to gain by revolution; and during the Mutiny of 1857, such disaffection as had broken out in Bengal soon disappeared, and 'the Sepoys took to the villages and the jungles, and then they literally melted away before the impassive demeanour, the want of sympathy, and the silent loyalty of the zemindars.' In the second place, in years of scarcity and famine, which seem to recur periodically in India, the co-operation of the zemindars, both in raising funds and in carrying out relief operations, has been of inestimable value; and in the present distressful year the premier zemindar of Bengal has distinguished himself by a donation amounting to about £100,000.

Sir John Shore, afterwards Lord Teignmouth, succeeded Cornwallis as Governor-General, and ruled India from 1793 to 1798. Under his administration the Permanent Settlement was extended to the Province of Benares. But the current of peaceful reforms was now disturbed by the turmoil of war, which had already broken out in Europe, and which led to a change of policy in India. For about twenty years—from 1794 to 1815 in Europe, and from 1798 to 1818 in India—the record of peaceful reforms is poor; the annals are full of the incidents of war. Consistently with the plan which we have laid down for ourselves, we shall rapidly pass over these incidents, until we come again to a new period of peace and reforms.

Pre-eminently a peace Minister, Pitt avoided being

drawn into a war as long as he could. When the Revolution broke out in France in 1789, and the Bastille was taken, Pitt remained unmoved and firm amidst the wildest excitement. In 1790 Pitt wrote that England meant to persevere in the neutrality which it had hitherto scrupulously observed with respect to the internal dissensions of France; and even in 1792 Pitt hoped to keep England free from the war. But the public feeling in England was too strong for Pitt. After the events of August 10, 1792, the British Government recalled their Ambassador from Paris; and after the execution of Louis in 1793, they ordered the ex-Envoy of France to leave England, which virtually meant a declaration of war. France replied by an open declaration of war.

Into the events of the war, which continued for eight years, from 1794 to 1801, it is not our purpose to enter. The British Navy won renowned victories and swept the seas, but the British Army made only scattered, feeble, and ineffectual efforts. These feeble and ineffectual expeditions by land cost England no less than 60,000 men up to 1801, without securing any great advantages, and Macaulay therefore has some grounds for calling Pitt an incapable war Minister.

But Pitt's policy should be judged, not by the result of the expeditions he sent out to the Continent, but also by the great coalitions he formed against Napoleon; and if the coalitions, too, failed, it is because no human endeavours were then of any avail against that great genius of war. Napoleon demolished the first coalition by his brilliant Italian campaign, and Austria, the last ally of England, laid down her arms and concluded a treaty with the conqueror in 1797. The indefatigable Pitt formed a second coalition, arming Russia and Turkey, Naples and Austria, against France; and he even refused the First Consul's offers of peace, hinting that there could be no peace until 'the restoration of that line of princes which for so many centuries maintained the French nation in prosperity at home, and in consideration and respect abroad.' Napoleon sent his famous reply, alluding to the English revolution to which the Hanover line of kings owed the English throne; but his most effectual reply was given in the field of Marengo. The second coalition was demolished, and Austria concluded peace with France in 1801. Pitt resigned in the same year, after holding the post of Prime Minister for seventeen years, and England concluded the Peace of Amiens with France.

The two coalitions spoken of above had been secured by a vast expenditure of treasure. In 1795, and again in 1797, the British Exchequer guaranteed loans aggregating to over £6,000,000 in consideration of Austria maintaining her armies in war against France, and subsidies were also given amounting to over £9,000,000. The total addition made to the national debt of England during these eight years up to 1801 was the fabulous sum of over £334,000,000!

While Pitt made such vast sacrifices to maintain the war against France, his endeavours to crush every opposition at home were still more strenuous, and perhaps regrettable. The question of Parliamentary Reform which had engaged his attention in the earlier days of peace was shelved for ever, and the advocacy of such reform was now treated as a crime. In Scotland the Reform Party was persecuted and punished with appalling severity. Muir, a member of a convention with revolutionary aims, was transported for fourteen years. Palmer, a clergyman, was transported for seven years for circulating a paper in favour of Parliamentary Reform. Skirving, Margarot, and Gerrald were transported. In England the Habeas Corpus Act was suspended from 1795 to 1801. One Act enlarged the list of treasonable offences, and another Act forbade all public meetings of more than fifty persons without the superintendence of a magistrate. And regulations and restrictions were imposed upon the press. It is fair to Pitt to state that he rather yielded to the public sentiment than led it. 'The public in its terror called for more and more; Parliament passed every repressive measure with something like acclamation; it was not the coercion of a people by a Government, it was the coercion of a Government by the people.'*

If such things could take place in England, it may be imagined that the state of things was a hundred

* Lord Rosebery's 'Pitt,' p. 167.

times worse in Ireland. Between the Catholic Party, agitating for emancipation, and the Ulster Protestants there was a feud worse than war. There were murders and roastings on one side, there were picketing and scourging, hanging and house-burning, on the other. The French sent expeditions to Ireland in 1796 and again in 1798, and in the last year the Irish rose in open rebellion, and were repressed with cruel and atrocious severity.

Harassed by a war abroad, and probably more harassed by the state of things in Ireland, Pitt resolved on a great measure. Ireland must be united with England. There must be one Parliament, not two; and this must be effected by any means by which it was possible to secure the object. In 1799 the Irish Parliament rejected the propositions of the Government for a union. Then followed a system of coercion and bribing to secure the object. 'The corruption was black, hideous, horrible; revolting at any time, atrocious when it is remembered that it was a nation's birthright that was being sold.'* Out of 300 members, sixty-three were bribed or coerced to vacate their seats, and men favourable to the Union were elected, and the measure of Union was passed in 1800. 'The whole unbribed intellect of Ireland was opposed to it,' but the object aimed at was secured, and Ireland was united with England under one Parliament, so as to present a united front to the enemy.

* Lord Rosebery's 'Pitt,' p. 189.

We have dwelt at some length on these transactions in Europe because the history of India during the closing years of the eighteenth century and the opening years of the present century is unintelligible without a knowledge of Pitt's European policy. Lord Mornington, who ruled India from 1798 to 1805, was Pitt's friend and imitator. Before coming out to India, he had asked Pitt for a peerage of Great Britain, and Pitt had procured one for him by using his influence with the King. Arrived in India, Lord Mornington followed the policy of Pitt as closely as a European policy can be imitated in India. In 1799 Lord Mornington received the high title of Marquis Wellesley of Norragh, and when he grumbled that an English marquisate had not been conferred on him, he received a just but friendly rebuke from his patron and friend. In 1805 Wellesley was recalled from India, and reached England in time to see his dying friend. There is scarcely a more touching episode in the history of the times than the friendship between the great Commoner who swayed the destinies of England and the great Marquis who swayed the destinies of India. Death alone closed the friendship in 1806.

Pitt's engrossing idea was to unite Europe against the power of Napoleon. Wellesley's engrossing idea was to unite India under the paramount power of England against a possible invasion of the French. Pitt granted subsidies to European Powers to maintain armies in war against the common enemy. Wellesley modified this policy so as to make it suitable to the conditions of India. To grant subsidies to the Indian potentates, and to maintain their inefficient troops in readiness, would have been waste of money. He therefore obtained subsidies from those potentates in order to maintain British armies in their dominions. By this skilful adaptation of Pitt's policy he succeeded in uniting India under the supreme power of England.

The Nizam of Hyderabad had maintained some French battalions; Lord Mornington induced him to disband these battalions in 1798, and to receive and pay for a British force in his dominions. Tipu Sultan of Mysore had proposed to conclude an offensive and defensive alliance with the French. Lord Mornington resolved to crush this Mysore chief. An English army under General Harris marched on Seringapatam, the capital of Mysore. Tipu died like a warrior, sword in hand, in 1799, and the power of the house was extinguished for ever.

The fall of Mysore was followed by the fall of Tanjore and the Carnatic. Lord Mornington, now Marquis of Wellesley, dealt with both in his own arbitrary way. He deposed the reigning prince of Tanjore, and placed a rival on the throne, on the condition of transferring the entire administration to the British! And on the death of the Nawab of the Carnatic he allowed one of the rival heirs to succeed on condition of a similar transfer. The Raja of Tanjore and the Nawab of the Carnatic henceforth became political pensioners; their dominions passed under the administration of the British in 1801.

The Mahrattas were the only remaining power in India. Guided by the genius of the celebrated Nana Farnavis, they had declined to enter into any 'subsidiary' treaty, and Wellesley therefore waited for an opportunity to bring them to his snare. The opportunity came at last. In 1802 there were disputes between two claimants for the post of Peshwa, the head of the Mahratta confederacy. Baji Rao, one of the claimants, was worsted in battle, fled to the western coast, and saw nothing but ruin before him. In this extremity he signed the obnoxious treaty which the Mahrattas had declined so long, and agreed to receive a British force, if the British would help him to the coveted post of Peshwa. This was the celebrated Treaty of Bassein, signed on December 31, 1802.

Baji Rao was placed on the Peshwa's throne at Puna in 1803. The other Mahratta powers, Sindia, Holkar, and the Bhonsla, were staggered by this triumph of Wellesley's diplomacy, which introduced the British into the arena of their politics. War was the inevitable result, but into the details of this war it is needless for us to enter. Arthur Wellesley, afterwards the famous Duke of Wellington, crushed the power of the Mahrattas in the south in the celebrated battles of Assaye and Argaon; and Lord Lake defeated their army in the north, and entered Delhi, the ancient capital of

Hindustan, as a conqueror in 1803. From this date the British became the Supreme Power in India.

But Wellesley's troubles were not yet at an end. Sindia and the Bhonsla concluded 'subsidiary' alliances with the British, the former renouncing all claims to the regions north of the Chambal, and the latter ceding Cuttack and Berar. The Gaekwar of Baroda, another Mahratta chief, also ceded some territory for the maintenance of a 'subsidiary' force. But Holkar remained yet unsubdued, and while the war with Holkar was still proceeding, Sindia threw off his allegiance to the British, and joined Holkar, once more to uphold the common Mahratta cause. Thus complications began again; the East India Company were alarmed at the unending wars of Wellesley, and scarcely veiled their disapprobation of his action in their letters. But they retained the conquests while they disapproved of the wars, and Wellesley replied to them with cutting irony: 'The general fame of your equity and magnanimity would have precluded any supposition that in condemning the justice of our cause you would retain the fruits of our success, or enjoy the benefits of the peace while you repudiated the necessity and the policy of the war.' Wellesley was recalled in 1805.

We have seen before that Pitt's second coalition against Napoleon failed in 1801. Pitt retired from office, and the preliminaries of the Peace of Amiens between France and England were settled in the same year. But the peace was of short duration. War broke out again in 1803, and in the following year the English nation recalled to the office of Prime Minister the one man in England who had shown a capacity to continue it with tenacity of purpose, if not with success. Pitt took his seat in the House of Commons on May 18, the very day on which his great antagonist was proclaimed Emperor of the French.

Pitt's war policy was the same as before, but on a grander scale. He matured a gigantic alliance with the European Powers. Russia agreed to bring 500,000 men against France. Austria signified her adherence to the new coalition. Prussia was still hesitating, and had not yet joined, when the coalition was crushed.

Napoleon had collected his grand army at Boulogne, bent on striking a mortal blow at England, and was only waiting for his fleet. News came to him, however, that his fleet had retreated to Cadiz. News also reached him of the great coalition which England and Russia and Austria had joined, and which Prussia was about to join. There was not a moment to be lost; Napoleon changed his plans and marched into Austria. England heard with dismay that the Austrian General, with 30,000 veteran troops, had been surrounded at Ulm, and had surrendered to the great conqueror. A few days after, tidings of the victory of Lord Nelson at Trafalgar cheered the English nation, and Pitt's health was drunk as the saviour of Europe. But Pitt replied almost in pathetic terms, 'Europe is not to be saved by any single man.' How true these words were Englishmen knew, when they learnt a few weeks after that the invincible Napoleon had crushed Austria and Russia in the field of Austerlitz on December 2, 1805. The armies of Austria and Russia were scattered, peace was being negotiated, the third coalition against Napoleon was at an end. The news killed Pitt.

The last scene of the drama of Pitt's life is well known. Pitt was at Bath when the tidings of Austerlitz reached him. He opened the packet and was staggered. He asked for some brandy and swallowed one or two drams; had he not, he must have fainted. On January 9 he set out for home. As he entered his villa on the 12th, his eye fell on a map of Europe. 'Roll up that map,' he said; 'it will not be wanted these ten years.' Two days after, Wellesley, just returned from India, came to see Pitt, and had a long interview. This was the last interview that Pitt gave to anyone; he saw none but his family and physicians after this. He steadily declined, and on January 23 the greatest statesman of England was dead.

The death of Pitt made no change in the policy of England. His successors, Grenville and Portland and Percival and Liverpool, continued the war, and the genius of Wellington gave it a new turn in Portugal and in Spain. But it was Napoleon's fatal blunder in Russia which ruined his hitherto invincible army and caused his downfall. He hastened to Paris, raised a new army, and sustained his first great defeat at Leipzig. Never did even Napoleon's genius shine brighter than in his defence of France against the countless armies of Russia, Austria, and Prussia, but all attempts were unavailing, and the great Emperor abdicated and was sent to Elba. His return from that island, and the eventful 'hundred days,' ending in the final defeat of Waterloo, are among the most stirring and momentous events in modern history. His star was set, and the policy inaugurated by Pitt bore its fruit nine years after his death.

In India the unending wars of Lord Wellesley led to a reaction, and his successors, Cornwallis and Barlow and Minto, were for peace. But the problem which was left unsettled by Lord Wellesley became ripe for solution when Lord Moira came out as Governor-General in 1813. After the conclusion of a war with Nepal, the new Governor-General, now Marquis of Hastings, found himself face to face with the Mahrattas and the Pindaris.

Never had any war a more complete justification than the war of Lord Hastings against the Pindaris. They were professional freebooters, who had risen to power with the decline of the great hereditary houses of India, and now ravaged the country from the Jumna to the Coromandel coast. The cause of security and peace, the cause of civilization and progress, demanded the subjugation of these free-booters, and Lord Hastings made preparations on a scale hitherto unknown in India. Cornwallis had brought 30,000 men against Tipu Sultan, and Lord Wellesley had assembled 60,000 against the Mahrattas. Lord Hastings called together the armies of the three presidencies, which, together with contingent and irregular troops, numbered 120,000. The armies moved up from the north, west, and south, and closed round the enemy. The Pindaris were crushed in 1818, and mostly settled down as peaceful cultivators, and India knew no more of this race of plunderers.

The proceedings against the Mahratta powers were concluded about the same time. Baji Rao, who had first brought the British into the arena of Mahratta politics by the Treaty of Bassein in 1802, now chafed under the control of his new friends; and the other Mahratta chiefs were eager to join the common cause. But the gallantry of the British troops, European and Indian, strangled all opposition. Sindia yielded to British pressure, and concluded a treaty in 1817. Baji Rao attacked a small British force at Khirki with 18,000 horse in November of the same year, but was repulsed by Elphinstone and fled. The Bhonsla of Nagpore also attacked 1,400 Indian Sepoys with his 18,000 troops at Sitabaldi in the same month, but was repulsed and fled. Holkar's army murdered their Queen, who desired to be at peace with the British, and plundered the baggage of the British, but were crushed by Sir John Malcolm at Mehidpur in December. Baji Rao's dominions were annexed to the

Company's dominions in February, 1818, and now form the Bombay Presidency. And a few months after Baji Rao himself was arrested by Sir John Malcolm and retired as a pensioner. The power of the Mahrattas, who were virtually the masters of India for about a hundred years, from the time of the decline of the Moguls, was thus effectually crushed; and henceforth the English had no rivals in India east of the Sutlej.

CHAPTER II.

THE AGE OF CANNING AND GREY.

1815—1835.

It is a relief to turn from the annals of war, however glorious, to the annals of the peace which succeeded. It is a relief to turn from the account of battles and invasions to the account of those measures of reform and advancement which elevate nations and add to the happiness of mankind. And never was there any period when Europe and India made more real progress within the lifetime of one generation, than during the twenty years which succeeded the Napoleonic wars and the last Mahratta wars.

England had paid heavily for the Napoleonic wars. Her public debt had increased from £268,000,000 to the fabulous sum of £800,000,000. Her taxation had increased enormously, until in 1814 it had risen to £6 for each person in the country, a rate unknown upon the earth, excepting then. All proposals of Parliamentary Reform and of Catholic emancipation had been postponed, the Habeas Corpus Act had been suspended, and

Englishmen had submitted to coercive Acts the like of which have been unknown since then. All Liberal measures were suspended at home and abroad. Slavery flourished; and during the first seven years of the present century English ships conveyed annually across the Atlantic 40,000 negroes, one half of whom perished at sea or soon after landing. The British Parliament abolished the slave trade by two Acts in 1807 and 1811, but allowed slavery to continue.

The settlement of Europe which followed the battle of Waterloo was framed in this spirit. In the Congress of Vienna, the triumphant allies undid much of the good which had been effected by the French Revolution, and forced nations to submit to conditions they had outgrown. Italy was forced back under the hateful rule of Austria. In Germany every petty despot was reseated on the throne he had occupied before. Holland and Belgium were crushed together into one kingdom. Norway was annexed to Sweden. The old partition of Poland was confirmed, and a people numbering 15,000,000 were formally handed over to Russia, Austria, and Prussia.

'It was a severe disappointment,' says a learned and impartial historian, 'when the English Minister was seen joining Talleyrand in upholding legitimacy, and for the sake of that principle, and to preserve on its old lines the balance of European power, himself demanding the destruction of the liberty of Belgium and of Geneva, and calmly acquiescing in the absorption of much of

Saxony, the final division of Poland, and the destruction of Norway. . . . It was no use to ignore the fact that the French Revolution had given a great impulse to the ideas of constitutional freedom. Even the conquests of Napoleon, followed as they always were by democratic changes, had fostered these ideas in the very countries which had suffered most from them; and when it appeared that all hopes and promises of freedom were entirely illusory, insurrections of the deceived peoples burst out in several parts of Europe.'* For half a century the people struggled against the fetters which the Congress of Vienna had forged for them, and within half a century they broke the chains in most parts of Europe. France turned out the incorrigible Bourbons; Italy threw off the yoke of Austria; the petty despots of Germany were restrained; Belgium freed herself from Holland; Norway received an autonomous constitution.

But we must turn from this digression to the story of England. The harvest of 1816 was bad, and the price of wheat rose to 106s. the quarter. Factories were closed, iron furnaces blown out, coal-pits were shut up. Employment was scarce, misery pervaded the land, and acts of violence by bands of starving men were frequent. In the midst of this universal misery the demand for reforms was once more heard. The famous William Cobbett promoted the great movement, and his words

* Rev. Dr. Bright's 'History of England,' vol. iii. (1890), pp. 1370, 1371.

sank deep into the minds of the people. Hampden Clubs multiplied, and the voice of the people waxed powerful.

Lord Liverpool was the Prime Minister of England for fifteen years, from 1812 to 1827; but Lord Castlereagh, the leader of the House of Commons, was the real Minister. He was identified with the spirit of a repressive Government, and during the seven years after Waterloo he did much to repress popular movements and stifle reforms.

In 1819 the Manchester reformers held a meeting of 60,000 persons, and a military force was sent against them. Mounted yeomanry dashed among the defenceless multitude, and the meeting was dispersed. Mounds of human beings lay on the ground, crushed down and smothered; and men, women, and children were carried from the field, killed or injured. This was followed by the famous six Acts passed by the Parliament. Englishmen were not to assemble in larger numbers than fifty. Magistrates obtained large powers to search houses suspected to contain weapons. Military exercises were forbidden. Newspapers were restrained. The movements for reform were restrained for a time—for a time only.

Castlereagh destroyed himself in 1822. The country did not grieve at his death; and when he was buried, the mob of Westminster cheered in triumph. He was succeeded as leader in the House of Commons by the noble-minded Canning, a great statesman, a gifted orator, a true Liberal at heart. His appointment as leader of the House of Commons, under Lord Liverpool, who was still Prime Minister, marks a turning-point in English history, and is the first official recognition of that Liberalism which was growing in England. Reforms, which had been delayed so long, came trooping in. The barbarous criminal laws of England, which inflicted the punishment of death on slight offences, were being slowly modified : a hundred felonies were exempted from capital punishment in 1823. The equally barbarous laws which kept the working classes bound as serfs to the British soil, and in convenient subordination to their employers, were repealed in 1824, and combinations of workmen to obtain better wages were no longer forbidden. Last, though not the least, was the subject of the emancipation of the Catholics, who were still debarred from sitting in the House of Commons or holding important offices under the Crown. Canning nobly fought for the complete emancipation of Catholics from all disabilities.

Nor was Canning's foreign policy less glorious. He checked the three despotic Powers of Europe—Austria, Russia, and Prussia—who had formed what was called a Holy Alliance, and had taken up an attitude of hostility against reforms. He recognised the independence of the South American colonies, Buenos Ayres, Mexico, and Columbia, and thus 'called the new world into existence to redress the balance of the old.' And he strove for the independence of Greece, until, in 1827, a treaty was concluded, to which France was a party, converting Greece into a self-governing country —an autonomous vassal State under Turkey.

Lord Liverpool died in 1827, and Canning now became Prime Minister. High expectations were entertained from his tenure of office, but fate willed otherwise. His Ministry was scarcely fully formed before Canning died, in August, 1827. But the good causes for which he had fought triumphed. The Catholic Emancipation Bill was passed into law in 1829, and the complete independence of Greece was recognised by Europe in 1830.

George IV. died in 1830, and his death was followed in due course by a dissolution of Parliament. Before the polls were opened for a new election, news came that the French had expelled their Bourbon King, Charles X., and recovered their liberties under Louis Philippe. The news created a deep impression in England, and public meetings were held everywhere to express approval of the new Revolution in France. This universal feeling influenced the elections, and the new Parliament was decidedly in favour of reform. The French Revolution of 1830 directly led to the Revolution in the Netherlands, resulting in the separation of Belgium and Holland; and in England it hastened the Parliamentary reform which statesmen had been vainly trying to effect for nearly half a century.

The Duke of Wellington, who was Prime Minister after Lord Liverpool, was neither in favour of healthy popular revolutions in Europe nor of reforms in

England. Belonging to the school of statesmen who had worked in the Congress of Vienna for the settlement of Europe on the old basis, he never understood the progress of his time, and never looked with favour on popular movements.

When Lord Grey declared in the House of Lords that the country was looking forward to Parliamentary reform, the Duke haughtily replied that the country possessed a legislature which answered all good purposes, and that as long as he was a Minister he would resist all measures of reform. This was almost a menace; but the time had gone by when either the country or the Parliament would submit to it, even from the Duke of Wellington. Shortly after the opening of Parliament, the Government was defeated and resigned; and the Whigs, who had been excluded from power for nearly a generation, now triumphantly came to power. Lord Grey, the tried champion of reform, became Prime Minister, and it was understood and felt, in Parliament and all over the country, that the battle for reform was about to commence, and that the battle was not to end until the reform was effected.

On March 1, 1831, Lord John Russell introduced the Reform Bill in the House of Commons. It met with a tremendous opposition, and was read a second time by a majority of a single vote. Shortly after the Ministry sustained a defeat, and resigned. The Parliament was dissolved, and the country was called upon to pronounce its judgment on the Reform Bill.

The country spoke in no uncertain voice. The popular enthusiasm was irresistible. The Ministers secured an overwhelming majority in the new Parliament. Lord John Russell again introduced a Reform Bill on June 24, 1831, and its third reading was passed by a majority of over a hundred. The Bill was now sent up to the House of Lords, and its fate was watched with intense interest. Peeresses attended the House evening after evening to listen to the debate, and their daughters and relations were provided with seats below the bar. The space about the throne was thronged by foreigners; and among them sat the illustrious reformer, Raja Ram Mohan Rai, who knew how tenaciously the Brahmans of India defended their caste privileges, and who now witnessed with wonder how the Brahmans of England fought for *theirs*. The prolonged debates left no doubt as to the fate of the Bill; it was thrown out by a large majority on October 7.

For the third time within the same year, Lord John Russell introduced a Reform Bill in the House of Commons on December 18. It was finally passed without a division, but was lost once more in the House of Lords in May, 1832. Earl Grey now demanded of the King the power to create some fifty new peers to secure the passing of the Bill. The King refused, and the Ministry resigned.

Meanwhile, the excitement in the country had become intense. The congregation of the unions held, on May 7, a meeting at Birmingham, 150,000 strong, and their lofty union hymn declared their calm resolution to obtain their rights. They sang:

> 'God is our guide! no swords we draw,
> We kindle not war's battle-fires;
> By union, justice, reason, law,
> We claim the birthright of our sires.
> We raise the watchword, Liberty!
> We will, we will, we will be free!'

And, after the hymn was sung, every man of the 150,000 bared his head, and slowly and solemnly uttered the vow: 'With unbroken faith, through every peril and privation, we here devote ourselves and our children to our country's cause.'

Scenes like this were now frequently witnessed all over the country. Political unions met continually. A petition signed by 25,000 men at Manchester asked the House of Commons to grant no supplies till the Bill was passed. The Birmingham union, now 200,000 strong, held a meeting, and resolved to pay no taxes till the Bill was passed. The Common Council of the City of London declared that all concerned in stopping the passage of the Bill were enemies to their country.

Dark schemes of the use of force by the Government were suspected. The Duke of Wellington was understood to be pledged 'to quiet the country in ten days,' and an attempt at military government was looked for. The gates of the barracks at Birmingham were closed on a Sunday, and the soldiers sharpened their swords on the grindstone. They were supplied with ball cartridges, and were booted and saddled day and night.

But the people's voice triumphed. The King failed to form a Tory Ministry. Earl Grey returned to office with power to create as many new peers as were needed. The House of Lords did not wait for this humiliation. The Duke of Wellington and a hundred other peers, majestically sullen, walked out of the House, and withdrew from farther opposition to the Bill. The Bill became law on June 7, 1832.*

Down to the date of the Reform Bill the representative system in England was grossly imperfect and corrupt. Two-thirds of the members of the House of Commons were elected through the influence of peers and other influential men. Seventy members were returned from places which had scarcely any population. Old Sarum, with not a single inhabitant, sent up two members, and Gatton, with seven electors, also sent up two members, the right to appoint whom was valued at £100,000. Seats were offered for sale, and Hastings had been so often sold for £6,000 that her market price was fixed at that sum. The members who bought their seats sold their votes, and thus their outlay was made remunerative. The Reform Bill changed all this, and political power passed from the peers to the middle class.

Among the new members who took their seats in this first reformed Parliament was an ardent young

* It bestowed the privilege of the franchise in towns upon occupants who paid a rental of £10; in counties upon those who paid a rental of £40.

man of twenty-three, who was destined to take an important share in the transactions of the Parliament and the country for sixty years to come: we mean Mr. Gladstone.

The years which followed were years of activity in the direction of reforms and of Liberal legislation, but it would be travelling far out of our province to narrate all these reforms, and we must therefore content ourselves with a bare mention of the more important measures. The most glorious work of the reformed Parliament was the abolition of slavery. In the West Indian possessions of Great Britain there was a slave population numbering 600,000. Clarkson, Wilberforce, and Buxton had aroused the national conscience on the subject, and the time had come for wiping out this blot on English history. The abolition of slavery was decreed in 1833, and a compensation of £20,000,000 was granted to slave-owners.

Other reforms were then taken in hand. Education was in a backward state in England, and in 1833 there was one person in eleven of the population attending school. A small grant was now made to promote national education. The employment of children in factories was restricted in the same year. The laws which encouraged lazy pauperism, and discouraged honest industry, were reformed in 1834. The heavy and prohibitive tax of fourpence on each copy of a newspaper was reduced to a penny, and the fetters on journalism were thus knocked off in 1836. Criminal laws were further modified. In 1837 was formed the Anti-Corn-Law League, whose work, promoted by the ever-memorable Cobden and Bright, bore fruit in the abolition of corn laws nine years after. And in 1837 a young Queen ascended the throne of England.

We have now narrated, as briefly as we could do it, the story of progress in England during the eventful years between the battle of Waterloo and the accession of the Queen to the throne. It was needful that this story should be told, however briefly, as the history of India during this period is unintelligible without a reference to English history. The same spirit of reform, and the same desire to promote the happiness of the people, marked the policy of England and of India during this progressive age; and the noble and liberal-minded statesmen who guided the destinies of England during this age, worked side by side with statesmen equally great and large-hearted, who ruled the destinies of India. To try to read Indian history apart from English history would be an endeavour to understand a result without knowing the cause. The same moving force determined events in both countries; the extension of privileges to the people of India during this period is the counterpart of the Reform Act in England; and Munro, Elphinstone, and Bentinck were inspired by the same reforming spirit and the same desire to benefit humanity as Canning, Grey, and Lord John Russell. To the story of India, therefore, we now turn.

We have referred before to the administrative reforms which were introduced by Lord Cornwallis. But his measures, judicious and liberal in their conception, were vitiated by one mistake. He had found the administrative officers of his time, both Europeans and Indians, self-seeking and corrupt. He purified the European service by increasing the pay of officers and elevating their status; but, on the other hand, with an Englishman's prejudices, he regarded the Indians as altogether unfit for judicial and administrative work, and excluded them from all real share in the task of administration. The results of this exclusive policy were disastrous.

We may accept it as an axiomatic truth that no great and civilized country can be successfully ruled by foreigners without the co-operation of the people. But Hastings and Cornwallis had forgotten this great truth. And 'it seems also to have been forgotten that for centuries prior to the introduction of European agency, law and justice had been administered solely by natives; yet society had been held together, and there had been times when, according to the testimony of travellers and historians, India had been populous and flourishing, the people thriving and happy.'* The powerful landlords of Bengal had been charged with the task of repressing robbery, violence, and crime within their estates; Hastings and Cornwallis deprived

* Mill and Wilson's 'History of British India' (1858), vol. vii., p. 280.

them of this power, and placed it in the hands of European judges. Elsewhere the village communities had maintained peace and repressed crime within villages; but this old institution had also been disorganized by the advent of the British rule.

Lord Wellesley was occupied with constant wars, and could pay little attention to internal administration. After him Lord Cornwallis came a second time to India in 1805, but died in the same year, and during the short rule of Sir George Barlow, who succeeded, little was effected. Lord Minto then came to India and ruled the country from 1807 to 1813, and during his administration the unwisdom of the exclusive policy began to be manifest in the increase of crime all over the country.

Robbery increased to a fearful extent, life and property in the British dominions became unsafe, and the country was kept in perpetual alarm. Writing in 1810, Lord Minto himself recorded in a minute that 'a monstrous and disorganized state of society existed under the eye of the supreme British authorities, and almost at the very seat of that Government to which the country might justly look for safety and protection. The mischief could not wait for a slow remedy; the people were perishing almost in our sight; every week's delay was a doom of slaughter and torture against the defenceless inhabitants of very populous countries.' A violent remedy was accordingly sought for and adopted. Actuated by that exclusive policy which still found favour with the Government, two European Superintendents of Police were appointed, one for Bengal and one for the Upper Provinces, with vast powers to arrest on suspicion and on the suggestion of informers. The remedy was almost worse than the evil. Inhabitants of villages were indiscriminately arrested on insufficient or false information, and detained in gaol for long periods without trial. In one district in Bengal 2,071 persons were arrested between May, 1808, and May, 1809, and remained in gaol for about two years without a trial. Many died in prison.

It then began to dawn on some of the ablest of the Company's servants that an efficacious administration of justice in India was only possible by allowing a real share of the work to the people of the country. Sir Henry Strachey, Circuit Judge of the District of Calcutta, declared: 'In a civilized populous country like India, justice can be well dispensed only through the natives themselves.' And Colonel Munro of Madras, who knew the people of India probably better than any of his contemporaries, asserted the truth, which was then almost a heresy to most of the Company's servants: 'If we pay the same price for integrity, we shall find it as readily amongst natives as Europeans.'

Lord Minto was succeeded by the Marquis of Hastings in 1813, as we have seen before, and it was during his administration that the principle advocated by Munro was gradually adopted in practice. Thomas Munro had come out to India at the early age of nineteen in 1780, when Warren Hastings was waging his wars against Hyder Ali of Mysore. A prolonged period of settlement work gave him ample opportunities for displaying that sympathy for the people and jealous regard for their rights which distinguished this noble-minded Scotchman, and it also gave him a thorough insight into the life and manners and institutions of the Indian villager. Like most Europeans who have mixed with the people in their homes, and not merely in the precincts of law-courts, he formed a favourable opinion of their simplicity, their integrity, and truth. 'They are simple, harmless, honest,' he wrote, 'and have as much truth in them as any men in the world.'

In 1814, after a stay of six years in Europe, Munro was again sent out to India by the Court of Directors as Principal Commissioner for the revision of the internal administration of the Madras territories. It would be beyond the scope of the present work to narrate in detail the work performed on this occasion; but the regulations which he recommended, and which were passed in 1816, are a monument of his high statesmanship and his deep sympathy for the people of India. Briefly, the regulations extended the powers of native Indian judges, and thus the principal share in the administration of civil justice was transferred to them. An attempt was also made to maintain and legalize the village *Panchyets* and to invest the headmen of villages with power to dispose of simple suits; but this plan eventually failed, as such village institutions cannot survive when the people are permitted at the same time to take their causes to higher courts. One retrograde step was taken, in transferring the functions of the magistrate from the judge to the revenue-collector, and thus combining judicial and executive functions, which had been separated by Lord Cornwallis. This step was possibly required by the circumstances of the times; after a lapse of eighty years, this combination of different functions is a source of much irritation and well-grounded complaint in India.

In the Mahratta War, which followed shortly after, Munro acted in a manner which commanded the admiration of his comrades in arms in India, and of high authorities in England. Sir John Malcolm, who had himself taken a prominent part in that war, as we have seen before, writes with genuine admiration of Munro's plan and operations:

'Insulated in an enemy's country, with no military means whatever (five disposable companies of sepoys were nothing), he forms a plan of subduing the country, expelling the army by which it is occupied, and collecting the revenues that are due to the enemy, through the means of the inhabitants themselves, aided and supported by a few irregular infantry, whom he invites from neighbouring provinces for that purpose. His plan, which is at once simple and great, is successful in a degree that a mind like his could alone have anticipated. The country comes into his hands by the most legitimate of all modes, the zealous and spirited efforts of the natives to place themselves under his rule, and to enjoy the benefits of a Government which, when administered by a man like him, is one of the best in the world.'

The last sentence of the above extract contains the true secret of the British conquest of India and the maintenance of British rule in India. It is often stated that India has been conquered by the sword, and should be held by the sword. Administrators who have spent their lifetime in India know the hollowness of this statement. The people in India submitted to the British rule because it was infinitely better than that which obtained in India at the close of the last century. And the people of India are content to live under that rule because it is more liberal and advanced, affords better security to life and property, and gives greater scope to progress and advancement, than any other rule which it is possible to have at the present day. And Thomas Munro was one of those men who at an early day of the Company's rule gave it the beneficent character which it has assumed.

In the House of Commons the great Canning commended the action of Munro with his accustomed eloquence: 'He went into the field with not more than five or six hundred men, of whom a very small proportion were Europeans, and marched into the Mahratta territories to take possession of the country which had been ceded to us by the Treaty of Poona. The population which he subjugated by arms, he managed with such address, equity, and wisdom, that he established an empire over their hearts and feelings.'

In 1820 Sir Thomas Munro received a fitting reward for his long and meritorious service: he was sent out as Governor of Madras. In the following year he heard with sorrow and regret that Canning had resigned his office of President of the Board of Control. On that occasion he wrote a memorable letter to the great British statesman, in which he reiterated the convictions of his lifetime. We have room only for one extract:

'Our present system of government, by excluding all natives from power, and trust, and emolument, is much more efficacious in depressing, than all our laws and school-books can do in elevating their character. We are working against our own designs, and we can expect to make no progress while we work with a feeble instrument to improve, and a powerful one to deteriorate. The improvement of the character of a people, and the keeping them, at the same time, in the lowest state of dependence on foreign rulers, to which they can be reduced by conquest, are matters quite incompatible with each other.

'There can be no hope of any great zeal for improvement, when the highest acquirements can lead to nothing beyond some petty office, and can confer neither wealth nor honour. While the prospects of the natives are so bounded, every project for bettering their characters must fail; and no such projects can have the smallest chance of success unless some of those objects are placed within their reach for the sake of which men are urged to exertion in other countries. This work of improvement, in whatever way it may be attempted, must be very slow, but it will be in proportion to the degree of confidence which we repose in them, and to the share which we give them in the administration of public affairs. All that we can give them, without endangering our own ascendancy, should be given. All real military power must be kept in our own hands; but they ought with advantage, hereafter, to be made eligible to every civil office under that of a member of the Government.'

Lord Amherst succeeded Lord Hastings in 1823, and was engaged in a war with the King of Burma, which ended in the acquisition of the important provinces of Assam, Arracan, and Tenasserim in 1826. Sir Thomas Munro rendered much help in sending troops to this war, and received the thanks of the Governor-General. When on the eve of leaving India, ripe in years and in honours, Sir Thomas died of cholera on July 6, 1827, a month before the death of his great friend, George Canning, then Prime Minister of England. Nearly half a century before, Thomas Munro had first landed at Madras as a cadet, and after having worked his way there as an ordinary seaman, because he could not pay for his passage. How much is India indebted to that poor friendless seaman!

What Sir Thomas Munro did for Madras, Mountstuart Elphinstone did for Bombay. He had come out to

India in 1796, at the early age of seventeen, and in 1803 had the honour of riding by the side of the future Duke of Wellington at his great victories at Assaye and Argaon. So much was Arthur Wellesley impressed with the coolness of the young civilian, that he remarked that Elphinstone had mistaken his profession, and ought to have been a soldier.

Years passed on, and when the last Mahratta War broke out in 1817, Elphinstone was Resident at Poona. He understood Baji Rao much better than his friend Malcolm, but tried to maintain peace with him as long as he could. He left Poona just in time, and then beat back Baji Rao's 18,000 cavalry with his small force of less than 3,000 troops at the battle of Kirki, as has been stated before. Elphinstone's daring and successful resistance to the Peshwa was commended by George Canning in the House of Commons in the following well-chosen words:

'Mr. Elphinstone (a name distinguished in the literature as well as in the politics of the East) exhibited, on that trying occasion, military courage and skill which, though valuable accessories to diplomatic talents, we are not entitled to require as necessary qualifications for civil employment. On that, and not on that occasion only, but on many others in the course of this singular campaign, Mr. Elphinstone displayed talents and resources which would have rendered him no mean general in a country where generals are of no mean excellence and reputation.'

The Deccan was annexed to the British dominions in 1818, and then began Elphinstone's most arduous, and probably most memorable, work—the settlement of the Deccan.

We have said little about the settlement work of Munro in Madras, and we will say little of the settlement work of Elphinstone in Bombay. Land tenures in India are of a somewhat complicated nature, and the details of the settlements made with tenants in Madras and in Bombay will not interest the general reader. It is enough to state that in neither of those provinces was there a class of landed proprietors answering to the landlords or zemindars of Bengal; and settlements were accordingly made with the cultivators or ryots direct, after a survey of their holdings. This is known as the *Ryotwari Settlement*, as opposed to the *Zemindari Settlement* of Bengal; and Munro was practically the author of the Ryotwari Settlement. The principle was sound, but it was vitiated by one mistake.

In Bengal Lord Cornwallis had made a Permanent Settlement in 1793. High authorities had approved of this step, and promised its extension to other parts of India. The Marquis of Wellesley declared in Parliament, in 1813, that the situation of the natives of India had been ameliorated, and the rights of property secured, by the Permanent Settlement, the extension of which to other provinces was alone wanting to ensure its entire success. And Lord Grenville, agreeing with the Marquis of Wellesley, suggested the insertion in the new Act of a provision binding the Government of India to extend to the Upper Provinces the system introduced in Bengal. Nevertheless, when the time came, Permanent Settlement was not extended to any other provinces in India. The Governments of Bengal and Madras 'tenaciously adhered to the principle of permanency, and maintained that the interests of the Government and the expectations of the people, justified by previous promises and regulations, required that a settlement in perpetuity should be made, either immediately or after a brief interval. They were, however, positively prohibited from carrying the measure into effect without the previous sanction of the Court (of Directors), and, in obedience to these orders, the arrangement was indefinitely deferred.'* It was thus that the Upper Provinces of Bengal and the Province of Madras failed to obtain the benefits of a Permanent Settlement, and when Elphinstone concluded the settlement of the Deccan a Permanent Settlement was out of the question.

The result has been most unfortunate. Throughout Madras and Bombay, and the Upper and Central Provinces of India, the land revenue is increased at every settlement, and the condition of the cultivators has not improved, as it has improved in Bengal, with the improvement and extension of agriculture. Four-fifths of the population of India are dependent on land for subsistence, and in spite of every endeavour at

* Mill and Wilson's 'History of British India,' vol. viii., p. 360.

moderation, the assessments made at every new settlement mean an increased demand from the population of India. And it is not possible that the condition of the mass of the people in India will materially improve, or that they will be able to provide against droughts and recurring famines, until the constantly-increasing demand from the produce of land is permanently fixed.

In civil and criminal administration Elphinstone followed the principle adopted by Munro in Madras, and maintained the old village system as far as possible. The village head man, or *Patel*, maintained peace within the village, and could inflict light punishments for petty offences; and village *Panchyets* adjudicated civil suits. As in Madras, however, the *Panchyets* were neglected when the people were permitted to take their cases to higher courts, and this has not been an unmixed good for the country. And, lastly, the arrangements adopted in Madras for the union of police and magisterial duties in the hands of the revenue-collector was implicitly followed in Bombay.

In 1819 Elphinstone's meritorious services were rewarded by his appointment as Governor of Bombay, and he held that high appointment for eight years, from November, 1819, to November, 1827. How ably, how justly, and how sympathetically, he performed the duties of his post is known to every Indian, and has been described in a few words by Bishop Heber, who visited him in 1825. The Bishop writes:

'He is evidently attached to, and thinks well of, the country and its inhabitants. His public measures, in their general tendency, evince a steady wish to improve their present condition. No Government in India pays so much attention to schools and public institutions for education. In none are the taxes lighter; and in the administration of justice to the natives in their own languages, in the establishment of *Panchyets*, in the degree in which he employs the natives in official situations, and the countenance and familiarity which he extends to all the natives of rank who approach him, he seems to have reduced to practice almost all the reforms which had struck me as most required in the system of government pursued in those provinces of our Eastern Empire which I had previously visited.'

It is pleasant to read this account of a state of things which has unfortunately now passed away. With the increase of British population in Indian towns, and with the closer connection which now exists between India and England through steam and telegraph, the administration of India has improved in various ways; but it has deteriorated in one way. Englishmen now see less of real Indian life, and mix less with the Indian people than they did of old. The reign of affection is gone; the reign of law is come—of cold officialism on the one side, and of constitutional agitation on the other. The change had already commenced in Elphinstone's time, and that far-seeing statesman wrote feelingly of the change in speaking of Sir John Malcolm:

'Malcolm certainly has wise and enlarged views of policy; and, among them, the kind and indulgent manner in which he regards the natives—though perhaps originating in his heart as much as in his head—is by no means the least important. It appears to particular advantage in his feelings towards the native army, and in the doctrines he has inculcated regarding them. It is melancholy to think that he is not young, and that he is the last of the class of politicians to which he belongs. The later statesmen are certainly more imperious and harsher in their notions, and are inferior in wisdom, inasmuch as they reckon more on force than he does, and less on affection.'

One of the great acts of Elphinstone's administration after he became Governor of Bombay was the codification of the law. The task was twofold: firstly, to revise and reduce to system the existing regulations of the Bombay Council; and, secondly, to compile a digest of the customs and usages of the people. The first part of the work was well done, and the Bombay law was codified in twenty-seven regulations subdivided into chapters and sections. The second part of the work, in which Elphinstone took the utmost interest, was an attempt in advance of the time, and was never properly done.

The principal aim and object of Elphinstone's administration, however, was to ameliorate the condition of the people, and to raise their position and status, and to this object Elphinstone for ever remained true. In 1822 he wrote to Sir Thomas Munro, that, 'besides the necessity for having good native advisers in governing natives, it is necessary that we should pave the way for the introduction of the natives to some share in the government of their own country.' In 1824 he recorded, in his famous minute on education, that 'it may not be too visionary to suppose a period at which they (the natives of India) might bear to the English nearly the relation which the Chinese do to the Tartars, the Europeans retaining the government and the military power, while the natives filled a large portion of the civil stations, and many of the subordinate employments in the army.' And in 1826, in the year before he left India, he reiterated this opinion in a letter to Henry Ellis: 'It has always been a favourite notion of mine that our object ought to be to place ourselves in the same relation to the natives that the Tartars are in to the Chinese, retaining the government and military power, but gradually relinquishing all share in the civil administration, except that degree of control which is necessary to give the whole an impulse and direction.'

In November, 1827, a few months after the lamented death of his friend Sir Thomas Munro in the Madras Presidency, Elphinstone handed over the administration of Bombay to his equally esteemed friend, Sir John Malcolm. His acts still live in Bombay in the loving memory of the people, and the greatest educational institution in that town bears his name. In 1817 the

Hindu College was founded in Calcutta, mainly through subscriptions raised by the Hindus of Bengal; ten years after, in 1827, £27,000 was subscribed in Bombay, and the Elphinstone Institution was opened in 1834.

In the very year in which Sir Thomas Munro died in Madras, and Mountstuart Elphinstone left Bombay, Lord William Bentinck was appointed to succeed Lord Amherst as Governor-General of India. Bentinck's early career was checkered and eventful. At the age of twenty he had, as Lieutenant-Colonel of the 24th Light Dragoons, taken a part in the unfortunate campaign of 1794, in Flanders, against the French Revolutionary army, and seven years after he was with the Austrian army when it was defeated at Marengo by Bonaparte. In 1803 he had come to India as Governor of Madras, succeeding Lord Clive, the son of the conqueror of Bengal, but a mutiny in the army, which broke out three years after, led to his recall. We find him then in Sicily and in Italy, planning with the Duke of Orleans, afterwards Louis Philippe, King of France, for the emancipation of Italy; and after capturing Genoa in 1814, he restored to the Genoese their old constitution, and called on the Italians to struggle and be free. He was certainly one of the first Englishmen who conceived the idea of a free and united Italy; but the victorious allies wanted to keep up the old régime, and the Congress of Vienna forced Italy under the hated rule of Austria in 1815. Twelve years after this he was appointed Governor-General of India, and he landed in India in 1828, at the mature age of fifty-four.

To narrate all the events of Lord William's administration of seven years would be travelling beyond the scope of the present work. It is enough to state that he followed in Bengal the policy which had been inaugurated in Madras and Bombay by Munro and Elphinstone, and which was now the settled policy of England towards India. Nor was the policy merely dictated by sentimental causes; pecuniary reasons as well as the exigencies of efficient administration required that the natives of the country should take an important share in it. The systematic employment of natives of India in administrative offices was rendered necessary by the cost of a purely British administration, and by the inability of the Indian revenue to meet it. And it was by adopting this remedy, as well as many others, that Bentinck changed the deficit of a million into a surplus of two millions before he left India.

There were other memorable acts which Bentinck performed in India and for India. By his vigorous and persistent exertions, the perfidious system of murders known as *Thagi* was virtually stamped out in India. Against the advice of many eminent Orientalists, and at the supposed risk of creating a mutiny in the country, the Governor-General abolished the infamous rite of *Sati*, *i.e.*, of allowing widows to burn themselves on the funeral pyre of their husbands, which had crept in as a custom among the Hindus without any sanction in their ancient religion. And also against the opinions of Orientalists, Lord Bentinck, advised by Macaulay and Metcalfe, declared English to be the official language of India, and promoted and fostered English education among the people of India. English education has drawn the people of India closer to Europe and to the civilization of modern times; and, looking on the policy merely from a pecuniary point of view, English education has made the cheap administration of India possible.

It was while Lord Bentinck was ruling India that the charter of the East India Company was renewed in 1833, happily the same year in which the first reformed Parliament sat in Westminster. The new charter accordingly contains clauses in the liberal spirit which then animated the English nation, but, in justice to Lord Bentinck, it should be recorded that one of the most liberal clauses, relating to the admission of the natives of India to higher appointments, was inserted at the instance of that large-hearted statesman. Twenty years after the renewal of the charter, Sir Charles Trevelyan placed on record in his evidence before the Select Committee of 1853 the following opinion:

'To Lord William Bentinck belongs the great praise of having placed our dominion in India on its proper foundation in the recognition of the great principle that India is to be governed for the benefit of the Indians, and that the advantages which we derive from it should only be such as are incidental to, and inferential from, that course of proceeding.'

This is a great principle and a high ideal, and it cannot be said that England has always been able to act up to this ideal during the sixty years which have elapsed since the time of Lord William Bentinck. Nevertheless, it is a gain in the cause of good administration to strive after a great principle, and the principle that India should be governed for the benefit of the Indians has never been entirely lost sight of since the time of Bentinck.

It is, we venture to think, now clear to our readers that the marked progress in India between the date of Waterloo and the date of the accession of the Queen is intimately connected with, and is the result of, the progress in England during the same period. In both countries this period witnessed great and important concessions to the people. In both countries abuses were removed, the government was improved, and the wise principle of carrying on administration for the good of the people, and through the people, was recognised. And in both countries the progress of the mind kept pace with the reform of administration. The brightest literary period in England within the present century is the period between Waterloo and the accession of the Queen, when Byron and Shelley wrote their finest poems and Scott wrote his immortal novels, when Dickens and Macaulay and Carlyle and a host of other brilliant writers began their literary careers. And in India the period of Macaulay, Elphinstone, and Malcolm, of Tod and Grant Duff, of Bishop Heber and Horace Hayman Wilson, has never been excelled in literary culture. Nor was this culture confined to Europeans alone. Indians imbibed liberal ideas, co-operated with Englishmen in the cause of education and progress, and gave the first indications of that healthy modern literature which has been produced in the present century under British influence. Raja Ram Mohan Rai was the most brilliant product of this age of progress. He helped the cause of English education and of social progress, he gave his support to Lord William Bentinck in abolishing the cruel rite of *Sati*, he established a pure theistic Hindu Church in the midst of idolatrous surroundings, and he formed the Bengali prose of modern times. Raja Radha Kanta Deb was his rival, and was the great champion of orthodox opinions, and the great Sanscrit lexicon which he compiled remains still the best work of the kind. Poetry also received a great development, and Iswar Chandra Gupta, the master of a prolific and easy style of versification, formed a new school, which numbered many talented writers who have since greatly developed and beautified their native tongue. While such progress was made in the vernacular, the young men who flocked to the Hindu College, founded in 1817, came out with a warm and enthusiastic appreciation of Western thought and literature, which has had the most beneficent effect on the social, moral, and intellectual progress of modern India. And as English education spread in the country, the people of India became more and more fit to take a wider share in judicial and administrative work, for which Lord William Bentinck had opened the way.

Such are the far-reaching results of European progress on the advancement of India. Englishmen are familiar with the names of Brougham and Canning, of Russell and Grey, who led this progress at home. Nor should Englishmen cherish with less veneration or with less affection the names of those equally great and good men who spread the light of European progress and culture in the Far East, who recognised the natural rights of the people of India, who elevated their status, and who confided in their loyal co-operation in the cause of good government. Greatest among these, the people of India cherish the names of Munro, Elphinstone, and Bentinck.

CHAPTER III.

THE AGE OF PEEL AND PALMERSTON.

1835—1865.

At an early hour on the morning of June 20, 1837, two messengers of high degree came to Kensington Palace with a message of the highest import. The palace was wrapped in silence in the light of the morning, and it was with some difficulty that they obtained admission into a room. There they rang the bell once, twice, but were informed by the servant that her Royal Highness the Princess Victoria was asleep, and must on no account be disturbed. 'We are come,' replied the Archbishop of Canterbury and the Lord Chamberlain, for the messengers were no others, 'on business of State to the Queen, and even her sleep must give way to that.' In a few minutes the Queen came into the room in a loose white nightgown and shawl, her hair falling on her shoulders, tears in her eyes, but perfectly collected and dignified. And the Archbishop and the Lord Chamberlain summoned her to the most illustrious throne in the world.

The Prime Minister, Lord Melbourne, was summoned, and the young Queen met the Privy Council at eleven o'clock. 'Never,' says Charles Greville, 'was anything like the first impression she produced, or the chorus of praise and admiration which is raised about her manner and behaviour, and certainly not without justice.' Such were the golden opinions won on the first day of her reign by the Sovereign whose benign rule of sixty years has recently been celebrated, and of whom our children's children will say with perfect truth:

> 'Her court was pure ; her life serene ;
> God gave her peace ; her land reposed ;
> A thousand claims to reverence closed
> In her as Mother, Wife, and Queen.'

Lord Melbourne had succeeded Lord Grey as Prime Minister in 1834. With the exception of a few months, during which Sir Robert Peel had held the office in 1835, Lord Melbourne continued in that post; and he was well fitted to give the young Queen that friendly guidance which she needed. He attended on her with watchful and disinterested care, and there sprang up between the Minister and his Sovereign a mutual respect and affection which never faltered. Graceful in presence and fascinating in his manners, of a genial disposition towards his friends, and fair, and even generous, towards his opponents, Lord Melbourne was eminently fitted to conciliate all parties. With all these amiable qualities, however, Lord Melbourne was not a strong man; or, rather, his strength consisted in letting things alone. The enthusiasm which the Reform Act of 1832 had created had died away. Whig members of the old school were opposed to hasty reform, while ardent reformers were disappointed at the slow progress made. And while the Liberal camp was thus divided in opinion, Lord Melbourne allowed matters to slide, never taking things quite seriously, and checking the ardour of his colleagues by his apparent indolence. Indeed, Lord Melbourne studiously concealed all trace of seriousness in his official work; and earnest men who wished to engage his attention were filled with despair when they found the Prime Minister sprawling on a sofa, or balancing a chair, or blowing a feather about the room, in the midst of his work.

Difficulties of a serious nature arose shortly after the Queen's accession. In Canada there was open rebellion in 1837 and 1838, and Lord Durham, a man of advanced views but of impulsive character, was sent out as Commissioner. He advised that a national, as contrasted with a local, feeling should be fostered by the union of the separate provinces and races, and that the principles of self-government should be supported by extending the powers of the Colonial Parliament and the Legislative Assembly. Lord Durham was recalled in disgrace, through the influence of more moderate men; but a Canada Bill, based on his sound and excellent report, was passed in 1840, and saved that colony to England.

The question of slavery was not yet completely settled. A sudden change is always attended with troubles, and the postponement of complete emancipation, and the introduction of a temporary system of apprenticeship, had made things worse. There was disaffection in Jamaica, and Sir Robert Peel spoke, and Carlyle wrote, in support of the wrong course. The slaves were, however, emancipated in 1838, and a Jamaica Bill was passed, after considerable mutilation, in 1839.

Concession to Ireland was an item in the party programme of the Liberals; and a Poor Law, a Tithe Bill, and a Corporation Bill were passed after considerable difficulty. In England, the voters who had elected the reformed Parliament were disappointed with the slow progress made, and the declaration of the Liberal leaders, that they did not intend to push reform any further, gave rise to popular discontent and to what is known as *Chartism*.

The aspirations of the people found expression in a formula known as the People's Charter, which claimed five political points, viz., universal suffrage, vote by ballot, annual Parliaments, abolition of the property qualification for a seat in Parliament, and payment of members. A national petition, signed by over a million men, was submitted to the House of Commons; riots took place in different towns; and for a period of about ten years—from 1838 to 1848—Chartism made itself felt from time to time. The movement then died away, but one of the five political points has been accepted, and some others have been closely approached.

While the feeble Government of Lord Melbourne was grappling with these various difficulties, with an uncertain majority in the House, there was one member of the Government who certainly gave no indication of feebleness. Lord Palmerston had entered Parliament in 1807, the year after Pitt's death, and had been Secretary-at-War during those eventful years which witnessed the gradual downfall of Bonaparte. In 1830, when Lord Grey became Prime Minister, Palmerston became Secretary of State for Foreign Affairs, and he continued to hold that post under Lord Melbourne. Strong in supporting the influence and interests of England abroad, imperious and even self-asserting in his actions, he made his power felt, not only by foreign nations, but also by his colleagues. His vigorous but somewhat arbitrary policy sometimes committed England to acts of questionable wisdom in Europe, while in the Far East it led to more questionable wars and occasionally to disasters.

A jealousy of the growing influence of Russia influenced his policy throughout the period of his tenure of power, and as early as 1838 he endeavoured to revivify Turkey as a check on Russian power. In 1840 he contracted a Convention with three European Powers for armed interference in support of Turkey, and in the following year a treaty was concluded by which Egypt once more submitted to Turkey.

In China Lord Palmerston's policy led to a war. The Chinese had closed their ports against Indian opium, and this led to the war known as the Opium War. 'Reduced to plain words,' says the historian of 'Our Own Times,' 'the principle for which we fought in the China War was the right of Great Britain to force a peculiar trade upon a foreign people, in spite of the protestations of the Government, and all such public opinion as there was of the nation.' Mr. Gladstone denounced the war with indignation, but the war went on. The Chinese island of Chusan was captured, the British fleet proceeded to the mouth of the Pekin River, and a preliminary treaty was signed in 1841. The Chinese still persevering in their opposition, Ningpo was taken and Canton was threatened. The Chinese at last yielded, and signed the Treaty of Canton in 1842, throwing open five ports to the British trade, ceding Hong Kong, and paying a large indemnity.

In India the forward policy of England led to a serious disaster. Lord Auckland arrived in India as Governor-General in 1836, and the jealousy of Russia, which inspired Lord Palmerston's foreign policy in Europe, shaped also the foreign policy of India. The Shah of Persia had, by the advice of the Russian envoy, besieged Herat, but the appearance of a British force in the Persian Gulf induced the Shah to raise the siege. England's object was thus gained, and the gate to India was safe. But Lord Auckland proceeded farther. He deposed Dost Muhammad, the able ruler of Afghanistan, and placed Shah Suja on the throne, with the support of a British army, in 1840. The Afghans remained quiet for a time, a false confidence was bred, and a part of the British army was sent away from Kabul. But the storm broke in the following year. The British envoys were killed, and then followed the disastrous and fatal retreat of 4,500 troops and 12,000 camp-followers from Kabul, pursued by the vindictive and triumphant Afghans. The sepoys, without proper clothing or shelter in an Afghan winter, entered the defiles between Kabul and Jellalabad. Thousands of them were killed by the volleys of their pursuers, or died of hunger and privations, and fell down on the snow never to rise again. Of the entire body of over 16,000 men, only one solitary survivor reached Jellalabad to tell the tale of the humiliation and disaster.

Lord Ellenborough succeeded Auckland in 1842. A British army of retribution was forthwith sent to Afghanistan, the Afghan chief was defeated, and Kabul was reoccupied. The great bazaar of Kabul, with its artistic structures, was blown up by the conquerors, but they wisely decided not to leave a force in Kabul again. Dost Muhammad, who had been living in India, was reseated on the throne of Kabul, and the British army returned to India.

Shortly after the conclusion of the Afghan War, Lord Ellenborough annexed Sindh to the British dominions, an act the justice of which was questioned at the time by Major Outram, and has never been fully vindicated. Ellenborough also reduced the army of Sindia's state, and settled matters satisfactorily in Holkar's dominions. Far more important, however, than these military transactions which historians love to narrate, was the great work of the land revenue settlement of the North-Western Provinces of India, which was carried out about this time, but which writers on Indian history scarcely stop to mention.

We have seen that in Bengal the settlement was made with landlords, and that in Madras and Bombay it was made with the tenants direct. In the North-Western Provinces the village-community system was found to be in a more perfect state than in Bengal, and it was wisely decided, therefore, to take the village or Mahal as the unit for the settlement of revenue, and settlements were thus made with villages, instead of with either landlords or tenants. This North-Western system is called the *Mahalwari Settlement*, and the first regular Mahalwari Settlement of the North-Western Provinces occupied no less than sixteen years, from 1833 to 1849. The authorities were now dead against a Permanent Settlement; the settlement in the North-Western Provinces was therefore made for thirty years, and the excessively high rate of two-thirds of the rental was demanded and obtained as the Government revenue.

We have remarked before that the English rulers of India have always found it more difficult to organize a wise system of civil administration than to defeat Indian armies in the field, and the present case is an instance in point. A demand of two-thirds of the rental caused more real hardship to the people at large than all the military transactions within the lifetime of the generation, and the hand of the British tax-gatherer was felt by the village communities as heavier than even the tyranny of previous rulers. After a bitter experience of many years, it was determined, in 1855, that the Government share should be reduced to one-half of the assets, but the proposal of a Permanent Settlement, raised again in 1860, was rejected. Each new settlement, therefore, sweeps away into the imperial treasury all the profits which the landed classes in other countries are permitted to derive from the rise of prices and the extension of cultivation, and a permanent improvement in the condition of the cultivating classes has thus become impossible in India.

In the Central Provinces of India a settlement was made, between 1835 and 1838, for twenty years, and two-thirds of the rental was claimed as the share of the Government. After the annexation of Nagpur and Berar by Lord Dalhousie, and after the Indian Mutiny which followed, a local administration was formed in the Central Provinces in 1862. A regular settlement was then made. The leading man in each estate or village, who collected rent from the tenants and paid it into the treasury, was recognised as the proprietor under the name of Malguzar; and the settlement made with him is known as the *Malguzari Settlement* of the Central Provinces.

To complete our account of land revenue settlements, which form the most important basis of British administration in India, we have only to add that a settlement was made in Oudh after the annexation of that province and the suppression of the Mutiny. The landlords of the province were known as Talukdars, and the settlement is therefore known as the *Talukdari Settlement* of Oudh.*

While these settlement operations, vitally affecting agriculture and the landed classes, were proceeding in the Northern Provinces of India, a great reform, in the interests of manufacturers and labourers rather than in those of agriculture, was carried after a strong and historic opposition in England. The Liberal Government of Lord Melbourne expired in 1841, Sir Robert Peel became Prime Minister for the second time, and he found himself face to face with the great question of

* It would be convenient to remember the five distinctive names for the five principal land systems in British India :

(1) The *Zemindari* system of Bengal, a settlement with landlords called Zemindars.

(2) The *Talukdari* system of Oudh, a settlement with landlords called Talukdars.

(3) The *Malguzari* system of the Central Provinces, a settlement with landlords called Malguzars.

(4) The *Ryotwari* system of Madras and Bombay, a settlement with tenants called Ryots.

(5) The *Mahalwari* system of the North-West, a settlement with villages called Mahals.

the abolition of the Corn Laws. The agitation had commenced with the commencement of the Queen's reign, and had gained force by the accession of Cobden and Bright, whose names are among the brightest among the bright names of the reformers of this century. The Corn Laws kept up the price of bread, and though this might be a gain to the landed classes, it caused hardship to manufacturers and labourers. And as England had already changed from a great agricultural to a great manufacturing country, it was obvious that the interests of the larger portion of her population required the abolition of the Corn Laws.

In 1842 Peel had somewhat modified the duties on corn, and reduced or abolished duties on 750 other articles which were taxed in those days. But the crisis came in 1845. The recent prosecution of O'Connell, the greatest of Irish leaders and the most beloved of Irish patriots, had caused a sensation in the country. The intense poverty and misery of the Irish tenants, under extravagant and grasping landlords, had been revealed by the Devon Commission, and had deepened the sense of wrong. Then came the failure of the potato crop in Ireland in 1845, which threatened a famine, and the crops of England and Scotland were also seriously injured. Peel himself belonged to the landed classes which were interested in keeping up the Corn Laws; but Peel was a Prime Minister and felt the high responsibilities of a Prime Minister. He could not reconcile himself to maintaining the Corn

Laws, which within a few weeks might bring on the country the horrors of a famine. Unable to convince his colleagues, he resigned.

But no other man in England was fit to guide the nation at the crisis, and Peel was recalled to his post. He returned, and proposed the total repeal of the Corn Laws. The Tories fiercely opposed the proposal, and Disraeli earned his fame by a bitter resistance to the proposed reform. On the other hand, Peel was supported by the whole strength of the Opposition, as well as by his more advanced followers. In this manner the Prime Minister triumphed against most of his party by a majority of nearly 100 on May 15, 1846. There was a danger yet in the House of Lords; but the Duke of Wellington, who was still the autocrat of that House, was wiser now than he had been at the time of the Reform Bill of 1832. With his usual candour, he said to his brother peers, 'You cannot dislike it more than I do; but we must all vote for it.' The Bill was passed.

And here we must take leave of these two eminent men—Peel and Wellington—who had exercised so profound an influence on the destinies of their country. The Tories regarded Peel as a deserter from their cause, and avenged themselves by out-voting him on another question, and Sir Robert Peel resigned. His closing words on leaving office in 1846 were almost pathetic. 'It may be,' he said, 'that I shall be sometimes remembered with expressions of good-will in the abodes of those whose lot it is to labour and earn their daily bread by the sweat of their brow. I trust my name will be remembered by those men with expressions of good-will when they shall recruit their exhausted strength with abundant and untaxed food, the sweeter because no longer leavened with a sense of injustice.' Four years after this Peel died, in 1850, from injuries received from a fall from his horse in Hyde Park. The eloquence of Mr. Gladstone in the House of Commons, and the tears of the Duke of Wellington in the House of Lords, testified to the universal feeling of the nation. Two years after this the great Duke himself passed away.

On the defeat of Peel, in 1846, a Liberal Government was formed, with Lord John Russell as Prime Minister; and Palmerston once more became Foreign Secretary. It was a year of terrible distress in Ireland, and the frequent and cruel evictions of tenants by landlords added to the misery of the people. Fair rent and fixity of tenure were the obvious remedies for the evil, but the influence of landlords was yet supreme, and no land legislation for Ireland was undertaken till after a quarter of a century. O'Connell, the great leader of the Irish, died in 1847. Fiercer spirits took the lead and gave darker counsels, while the distress of the evicted tenants became intense. On reading a report of the evictions and of the misery of the tenants, Sir Robert Peel exclaimed that he did 'not think the records of any country, civil or barbarous, presented materials for such a picture.' A rebellion broke out and was suppressed in 1848.

The year 1848 was a memorable year, not only in Ireland, but all over Europe. In France Louis Philippe was deposed and a republic was proclaimed, and the influence of the Revolution spread everywhere. In Italy the King of Sardinia invaded Lombardy to free it from the yoke of Austria. In Austria the great Hungarian patriot Kossuth rose in arms. In Prussia the King conceded the demands of reformers. In Germany the supporters of German unity established a National Assembly at Frankfort. But these ardent movements did not lead to immediate results. The Sardinians were defeated in the battle of Novara in 1849, and the dream of Italian independence was given up for a time. In Germany the effort towards unity broke down. The rising of the Hungarians was crushed by Austria, aided by Russia, with a cruelty which was a shame to civilization. 'The Austrians,' said Lord Palmerston, 'are really the greatest brutes that ever called themselves by the undeserved name of civilized men.' Palmerston sympathized with the movements of the people, but would not render them any active help; and he was charged in Parliament, not without reason, with intermeddling with revolutionary tendencies without dreaming of supporting his advice by war. Palmerston made the memorable reply that 'there are two objects which England ought particularly to aim at—the one is to maintain peace; the other is to count for something in the transactions of the world.'

The step which Palmerston took shortly after 'to count for something' was not a happy one. The house of a Maltese Jew, a British subject, was sacked by the mob of Athens, and the Jew demanded compensation from the Greek Government. Lord Palmerston supported this claim, and sent the British fleet to the Piræus to enforce the claim, and the Greek Government yielded in 1850. Such coercive action against a small Power, for reasons which were almost ridiculous, was unworthy of a great Power, and was naturally criticised in the House of Commons. Mr. Gladstone made a magnificent speech, in the course of which he exclaimed: 'It would be a contravention of the law of nature and of God if it were possible for any single nation of Christendom to emancipate itself from the obligations which bind all other nations, and to arrogate, in the face of mankind, a position of peculiar privilege.' This charge was powerful and just, but Lord Palmerston knew the prejudices of his hearers, and he rose to the occasion. He spoke for five hours, 'from the dusk of one day to the dawn of the next,' with all his wonderful vigour and skill. He defended the principles on which he had acted in every point; and he asked his hearers whether those principles 'are proper and fitting guides for those who are charged with the government of England; and whether, as the Roman in days of old held himself free from indignity when he could say, *Civis Romanus sum*, so also a British subject, in whatever land he may be, shall feel confident that the watchful eye and the strong arm of England will protect him against injustice and wrong.' Although opposed by Peel and Disraeli and Gladstone, Lord Palmerston carried his hearers with him. *Civis Romanus* settled the business, and the vigorous Foreign Minister secured a majority of fifty-six in support of his policy.

Probably this signal triumph rendered Lord Palmerston still more arbitrary than before, still more reliant on his own opinion and policy, in disregard to the wishes of the Cabinet and of the Queen. In 1851 Louis Napoleon treacherously overturned the French Republic, broke down all opposition, massacred the citizens who resisted and who did not resist, and waded through the blood of his countrymen to supreme power. There was a strong feeling in England against his conduct, and the Queen desired that the British Ambassador at Paris should take no part in the transactions. Great was her surprise to learn that the Foreign Minister had already expressed his entire approval of the action of Napoleon. Some correspondence followed, and Palmerston was dismissed from his office. But Lord Russell's Government survived this incident only by a few months. Palmerston succeeded in defeating the Government over the Militia Bill, the Ministry resigned in February, 1852, and Lord Derby succeeded as Prime Minister.

While these events took place in England, Palmerston's masterful policy was shaping the foreign policy of India. Sir Henry Hardinge, one of the heroes of the Peninsular War, had succeeded Ellenborough as Governor-General in India in 1844, when Peel was Prime Minister of England, and was forced to carry on one of the most memorable wars of modern India. The great Ranjit Singh had freed the Punjab from the Afghan yoke, and had made the Sikhs the greatest native power in India; but he had the wisdom to recognise the greatness of England, and had remained true to his treaty with her. But when his controlling wisdom and restraining hand were withdrawn by death in 1839, there was no power left in the Punjab which could manage the mighty and disciplined Sikh army. Dhalip Singh, the son of Ranjit, was a boy; the regent mother and her favourites were afraid of the Sikh soldiery; and the traitors who wielded the power of the State sought to save themselves by launching the formidable battalions on British territory. In November, 1845, 60,000 Sikh soldiers crossed the Sutlej, and thus hurled themselves against that adamantine breakwater of British power against which every successive Indian power had hitherto striven fruitlessly, and only dashed itself to pieces.

Two battles, such as the British had never yet fought in India, were fought in December. In the second of these engagements British cannon, says an eye-witness, were dismounted and the ammunition blown into the air, British squadrons were checked in mid-career, and battalion after battalion was hurled back with shattered ranks. But the enemy's position was finally carried after sunset. Two more battles followed in January and February, 1846, the last, at Sobraon, being the hardest-fought battle in the history of British India. The treacherous leader of the Sikh army fled at the first assault, and broke the bridge behind the army, but the army fought with the valour of heroes and the enthusiasm of Crusaders. The British won at last, but the victory was dearly won with the loss of more than 2,000 troops killed and wounded. The power of the Sikhs was, however, broken for a time, and a peace was concluded by which the British frontier was extended from the Sutlej to the Ravi, and the Sikh army was reduced.

Lord Hardinge was succeeded by Lord Dalhousie in 1848, and there was trouble yet in store for him. He was forced into a fresh war with the Sikhs in the first year of his administration, and the war was concluded in two sharp engagements. At Chilianwalla the British commander, Lord Gough, rashly tried to carry the Sikh intrenchment in the evening, and was defeated in his endeavour, with the loss of over 2,400 officers and men. The news of the disaster was received with astonishment and anger by Englishmen all over the world. Englishmen were unused to defeat, and never had English arms sustained such a reverse in the open field in India. A cry rose in England for the removal of the General, and Sir Charles Napier, the conqueror of Sindh, was appointed in his place. But Lord Gough had retrieved his reputation in the meantime by crushing the Sikhs at Gujrat, and the Sikh War was concluded. The question then arose whether the kingdom of Dhalip Singh, a minor, should be annexed for the sins of the unruly soldiers. Lord Dalhousie decided the question in his own fashion, and annexed the province, declaring that he could not be turned aside from fulfilling his duty 'by a feeling of misplaced and mistimed compassion for the fate of a child.'

Lord Palmerston's influence was now in the ascendant, and other annexations followed thick and fast. British merchants and captains had been roughly treated in Burma, and this led to a Burmese War and the annexation of Pegu, or Lower Burma, in 1852. The Raja of Satara had died in 1848, adopting an heir on his death-bed, a custom which has been recognised in India during 3,000 years. Lord Dalhousie ignored the custom, and annexed Satara. The Raja of Jhansi died in 1853, and his widow desired to adopt an heir. Dalhousie declined to recognise the adoption, and annexed the State. The Raja of Nagpur also died in 1853. Lord Dalhousie refused to sanction the adoption of an heir, and Nagpur was annexed to the British territory.

The admirers of Lord Dalhousie have attempted to justify these proceedings by theories which provoke a smile in the unbiassed reader. To the unbiassed reader an open and undisguised conquest is less repulsive than annexations made under the cover of specious sophistry. The only true defence which Dalhousie's conduct admits of is the defence made by the learned and philosophical writer of the 'Expansion of England.' The deeds of Dalhousie are as difficult to justify, says the impartial writer, as the seizure of Silesia or the partition of Poland. 'But these acts, if crimes, are crimes of the same order as those of Frederick—crimes of ambition, and of an ambition not by any means selfish.'*

Lord Dalhousie also obtained Berar from the Nizam of Hyderabad for the maintenance of the Nizam's contingent, and added it to the British dominions. And Dalhousie's last act in India was the annexation of Oudh, which had been under misgovernment for many years. Oudh was added to the British possessions on February 13, 1856, and on the 29th of the same month Lord Dalhousie made over charge of his duties in India to his successor, Lord Canning.

We turn with pleasure from Dalhousie's annexations to those great public works and educational measures with which Dalhousie's name is more pleasantly connected. Before he went out to India, Lord Dalhousie had, as President of the Board of Trade, a great deal to do with the extension of the railway system in Great Britain; and he was virtually the father of railways in India. He pushed on the work so vigorously that

* 'The Expansion of England,' by Sir J. R. Seeley, K.C.M.G., p. 315. London: Macmillan and Co., 1895.

before the end of 1856 thousands of miles were under construction or survey. Dalhousie also threw the ports of India open to the world, and during his administration the export of raw cotton increased from £1,500,000 to over £3,000,000, and the export of grain from less than £1,000,000 to near £3,000,000. The advantages which India has derived from the facilities afforded to communication and export are acknowledged on all hands. But the impartial historian is bound, in the interests of truth, to note some consequences which have ensued, and which are not generally noted. The manual industry of India cannot compete with the steam and machinery of England. And the facilities afforded to trade have, within the memory of men still living, killed the weaving and other old industries of India, and forced millions of artisans to the labour of the field or other humble pursuits.

Dalhousie also introduced the telegraph system in India, and, following on the lines of the universal penny postage of Great Britain and Ireland, he introduced the half-anna postage in India. Another of Dalhousie's beneficial acts was to give effect to Sir Charles Wood's famous despatch of 1854 on education. English education had been sanctioned in India by Lord William Bentinck; Sir Charles Wood's despatch made the vernaculars of India the steps which led up to English education. In the year after Lord Dalhousie left India, Acts were passed establishing three Indian Universities, which have since been increased to five, and these five Universities and numerous schools and colleges are now educating nearly 5,000,000 of pupils in India.

But we must hasten now to those great events which absorbed public attention during the momentous years of 1854 to 1857. After the fall of Lord Derby's Ministry in December, 1852, Lord Aberdeen became Prime Minister, Lord Palmerston became Home Secretary, and Mr. Gladstone became Chancellor of the Exchequer. Mr. Gladstone was now indispensable in this office. In the previous year he had exposed Mr. Disraeli's unfortunate Budget, and had replied to his taunts and sarcasms, with a dignity, ability, and power which marked him out as the foremost authority in England on finance. And in 1853 he introduced his own Budget in a speech of five hours, which held the House spell-bound, and which astonished and gratified the country.

'Here was an orator,' says Mr. Gladstone's biographer, 'who could apply all the resources of a burnished rhetoric to the elucidation of figures; who could make pippins and cheese interesting, and tea serious; who could sweep the widest horizon of the financial future, and yet stoop to bestow the minutest attention on the microcosm of penny stamps and post-horses.'* Public men and private friends joined in a chorus of eulogy; the Queen wrote to congratulate

* 'The Right Hon. William Ewart Gladstone,' by George W. E. Russell (London, 1896), pp. 117, 118.

the Chancellor of the Exchequer; and large classes of people felt that life was rendered easier and cheaper by Mr. Gladstone's Budget.

But the attention of all England was soon turned to another direction. Mr. John Bright was once walking with one of his sons, then a schoolboy, past the Crimean Monument in London. The boy caught sight of the solitary word 'CRIMEA' inscribed on the monument, and asked his father what it meant. John Bright made the emphatic reply, 'A CRIME.' It is not our object here to discuss Mr. Bright's opinion, or to inquire if the war was a crime; but it is necessary to mention that England drifted into that war without intending it and clearly knowing why, and that England lost 24,000 of her brave soldiers, and added £41,000,000 to her national debt, in order to support and prolong misrule in Europe.

Aberdeen wished and intended to avoid the war; but Lord Palmerston was as jealous and mistrustful of Russia now as he had shown himself to be in the first years of the Queen's reign. Although a Home Secretary, he exerted pressure on the Prime Minister, and forced the Government first into a close combination with the French Emperor, and then into acts which made the war inevitable. The demand of rival Churches for the custody of sacred places in Palestine, supported by France and Russia respectively, was followed by a claim on the part of the latter Power to a protectorate over all the Greek subjects of Turkey.

In July, 1853, Russia occupied the Danubian Provinces in support of this claim. The English and French fleets entered the Dardanelles in the following October, and war was formally declared in March, 1854. The incidents of the war are well known, and need not be repeated here. Aberdeen's Ministry fell as the war proceeded, and Palmerston, the principal author of the war, was called to the high post of Prime Minister of England in February, 1855. And Palmerston retained his post as Prime Minister from this date until his death in 1865, with a brief interruption of one year.

The Crimean War was concluded in 1856, and the peace which followed declared the neutrality of the Black Sea, to which all mercantile marines were to be freely admitted, but from which the ships of war of all nations were to be excluded. Persia had in the meantime found her opportunity, and had captured Herat; but she was compelled to withdraw from that town by a peace concluded in 1857. In China Lord Palmerston's action was of a more questionable nature. The capture by the Chinese authorities of the crew of a schooner called the *Arrow*, which was a Chinese vessel, but hoisted the British flag without any right, created complications, and eventually led to war. The causes of the war were so inadequate, and the proceedings were so unjust, that the House of Commons passed what was virtually a vote of censure. But Lord Palmerston was the idol of the nation; he dissolved the Parliament, and was returned by a triumphant majority.

Dark clouds had in the meantime gathered on the Indian horizon, and the Indian Mutiny broke out in 1857. It is not our purpose in the present work to examine the causes of that great outbreak, or to narrate the incidents of the war, which have been fully told by many able writers. There can be no doubt that Lord Dalhousie's hasty and unjust annexations had ranged influential chiefs against the British power in India, and had spread a well-founded alarm among others, whose turn might come next. These men found the sepoy an easy instrument in their hands, and the introduction of the Enfield rifle in the place of the old 'Brown Bess' enabled them to whisper a story that the British Government intended outrage on the religion of the Hindu and the Musalman alike by the use of a cartridge greased with the fat of the hog and the cow. The alarm spread like wildfire; sepoys broke out in open mutiny; and the whole country was in flame.

Then followed deeds of horror and of cruelty, on one side as on the other, which need not be narrated in this work. In the words of an impartial historian, whom we have quoted before: 'The contest seemed to lie between two savage races, capable of no thought but that, regardless of all justice or mercy, their enemies should be exterminated. Deeds of cruelty on one side and the other were perpetrated, over which it is necessary to draw a veil, and a spirit of bloodthirsty recklessness was exhibited which, in calmer times, fills the mind with horror.'*

It is our pleasing duty to record that, in the midst of the storm of anger and indignation which raged among Englishmen in India at this period, there was one man who remained true to the dignity of his post and to the principles of British justice. Lord Dalhousie was succeeded in 1856 by Lord Canning, son of the great George Canning who had virtually guided the affairs of Great Britain from 1822 to 1827, and had fought for the emancipation of the Catholics and the independence of Greece. When the son of such a father was appointed Governor-General of India, and was entertained by the Court of Directors at a banquet, he uttered those memorable and almost prophetic words which have now become historic: 'I wish for a peaceful time of office; but I cannot forget that in our Indian Empire that greatest of all blessings depends upon a greater variety of chances and a more precarious tenure than in any other quarter of the globe. We must not forget that in the sky of India, serene as it is, a small cloud may arise, at first no bigger than a man's hand, but which, growing bigger and bigger, may at last threaten to overwhelm us with ruin.'

When the great cloud arose, a year after Canning's arrival in India, Canning behaved as his great father

* Rev. Dr. Frank Bright's 'History of England,' Period IV. (London, 1893), p. 328.

might have behaved under similar circumstances. In the midst of almost universal frenzy, he remained unmoved. 'There is a rabid and indiscriminate vindictiveness abroad,' he wrote to the Queen in September, 1857, 'even among those who ought to set a better example. . . . Not one man in ten seems to think that the hanging or shooting forty or fifty thousand men can be otherwise than practicable and right.' 'For God's sake,' he wrote to Lord Granville about the end of the same year, 'raise your voice and stop this! As long as I have breath in my body, I will pursue no other policy than that I have been following: not only for the reason of expediency and policy above stated, but because it is immutably just. I will not govern in anger. Justice, and that as stern, as inflexible, as law and might can make it, I will deal out. But I will never allow an angry and undiscriminating act or word to proceed from the Government of India as long as I am responsible for it.'

This is noble, and almost sublime. But what is perhaps still more touching is his zealous fear for the reputation and good name of his countrymen, even at the very moment when they were assailing him with bitter invectives for his unfaltering moderation and justice. On one occasion, when the outcry against Lord Canning was bitter and vehement, he showed the Lieutenant-Governor of Bengal some papers illustrating the brutality of some of the special tribunals. The Lieutenant-Governor urged their publication, by way of reply to his calumniators. 'No,' said Lord Canning, locking up the papers in his drawer; 'I had rather submit to any obloquy than publish to the world what would so terribly disgrace my countrymen.' Such was the great Englishman who was at the helm of affairs in India in 1857, and by whom the Indian Mutiny was eventually quelled.

The Indian Mutiny sealed the fate of the East India Company. The great extension of the British Empire in India had suggested to thoughtful minds in England the desirability of bringing the administration directly under the Crown. It was felt that a Company which was originally formed of traders could not be the rulers of a vast empire. The power of the Company, too, had been reduced from time to time, and it was felt that no useful object was gained by keeping alive that venerable but purposeless institution any longer. The Indian Mutiny emphasized this feeling, and Lord Palmerston now introduced his India Bill, transferring the Government of India from the East India Company to the Crown. But the great Minister was not destined to carry out this measure; an unexpected incident drove him from office. An attempt was made against the life of the Emperor of the French, and it was discovered that the chief conspirator, Orsini, had prepared his plans in England. Lord Palmerston proposed to alter the law, and to make conspiracy to murder a felony. This appeared to the English nation an undue submission to French demands. The Bill was defeated in the House of Commons, and Palmerston resigned.

Lord Derby formed a Conservative Ministry in February, 1858, and prepared his India Bill, which, however, was a failure. It was then proposed that the principles should be discussed in the House, and that a Bill, the joint production of both parties, should be introduced. This was done, and the new Bill was passed in August, 1858. The East India Company ceased to exist, and their territories and powers were vested in the Queen.

On November 1, 1858, a great *Darbar* was held in Allahabad, and smaller *Darbars* were held in other district towns in India, in which the famous proclamation, announcing that the Queen had assumed the government of India, was read in the midst of the acclamations of the people. And elderly men in India still recall with pleasure, and narrate to their children, the spectacles which they witnessed forty years ago, connected with the transfer of India from the Company to the Crown.*

It was proclaimed then, in eloquent words, that justice and religious toleration would guide the Queen's

* The present writer has pleasant recollections of the *Darbar* in a Bengal district town which he attended on this occasion. Cheers from thousands of men accosted the message that the Queen had assumed the government of India; and Brâhmans held up their sacred thread and uttered a blessing which has come to be true—*Mahârânî Dîrghajîbî Haun*, *i.e.*, 'May the Great Queen live long.'

policy. An amnesty was granted to all who had risen against the Company's rule, except those implicated in murders. The Governor-General of India became also the Viceroy of India. Non-officials, European and Indian, were admitted to legislative councils to represent the wishes of the people. The Company's army was amalgamated with the Queen's army. The Sadar Courts of Calcutta, Bombay, and Madras were amalgamated with the Supreme Courts of those Presidencies, and were called High Courts. In the following year the pitiful plea by which Dalhousie had annexed so many Provinces was swept away, and the right of Indian princes and chiefs to adopt heirs on failure of natural heirs was recognised.

Many useful and beneficent measures were passed during the remaining years of Lord Canning's rule in India. The Indian criminal law was codified in that remarkable work at which Macaulay had assisted—the Indian Penal Code. The Civil and Criminal Procedure Codes were also drawn up. But important as these measures are, they sink into insignificance when compared with those greater measures which Lord Canning adopted to ameliorate the condition of the masses in India—the agricultural population. Lord Cornwallis had permanently settled the revenue which the Government demanded from the landlords of Bengal. Lord Canning passed the famous Act of 1859, by which he restrained the landlords from demanding undue enhancement of rents from cultivators. Thus the beneficent work of Cornwallis was completed, and the protection which had been granted by him to the landlords was extended to the cultivators.

Another noble and generous work was attempted by Lord Canning. A terrible famine desolated the North-Western Provinces of India in 1860. Such relief as it was possible to organize was organized; and when the calamity was over, the new Viceroy tried to seek out the true preventive for such calamities. To an earnest and sympathetic administrator like Canning the true remedy revealed itself at once. He marked that at each recurring land settlement the Government could increase its demand from the produce of the land. He marked that the extension of cultivation and improvement in the prices of crops could not, under such a system, benefit the Indian tenant as it would benefit the British farmer. He comprehended that under this system the people of India could save nothing, and could have nothing to fall back upon in years of bad harvest. And he had the courage to recommend that the Permanent Settlement, which had proved so beneficial to the people of Bengal, should be extended to other parts of India.

The Secretary of State for India accepted this wise and liberal view, and authorized Permanent Settlements to be granted to estates in parts of the country where a full and fair rate had been imposed under existing settlements. And he concluded his memorable despatch by describing the proposal as 'a measure dictated by sound policy, and calculated to accelerate the development of the resources of India, and to insure in the highest degree the welfare and contentment of all classes of her Majesty's subjects in the country.'

Had Lord Canning lived five years longer, India might have received the much-coveted boon. But the great statesman died in 1862, shortly after his return from India, and his large-hearted wisdom was not inherited by his successors. The proposal was discussed for twenty years, and finally abandoned in 1883. But the terrible famine which has overtaken the whole of Northern India in the present year will convince unbiassed and impartial judges that the decision of 1883 needs a revision, and that the remedy proposed by the first and greatest of India's Viceroys is the only remedy for bettering the condition of the mass of the people in India.

The beneficent administration of Lord Canning had a moral effect on the progress of the people, and we will pause for a moment to speak of their intellectual and moral culture during this period.

It was during Canning's administration that the great reformer and scholar of Bengal, Iswar Chandra Vidyasagar, undertook those social and literary reforms which have endeared his name among his countrymen. It was during Canning's administration that the greatest modern poet of India, Madhu Sudan Datta, composed his noble epic in the Bengal language. An Indian lawyer, Rama Prasad Rai, son of the eminent Ram

Mohan Rai of whom we have spoken in another chapter, was appointed a Judge of the newly-created High Court of Calcutta. The Civil Service of India had been thrown open to competition, and the first batch of Indian youths came to England to compete for this service during Canning's administration. One of them succeeded in the examination of 1862; other Indian students qualified themselves for the Bar; and the steady increase in the number of Indian students who have come to England during the last thirty years has drawn India closer to England, and has helped in the spread of English ideas among the educated classes of India.

Lord Elgin succeeded Lord Canning in 1862, but died in India in the following year. He was succeeded by Sir John Lawrence, who had saved the Punjab during the Mutiny. Lawrence's foreign policy has been well described as 'masterly inactivity,' a policy which Lord Palmerston himself was steadily pursuing in Europe during the closing years of his life. Lord Palmerston had become Prime Minister for the second time in 1859, after the fall of the Derby Ministry. Great events were now taking place in Europe and in America, but Lord Palmerston, whatever his sympathies might have been, declined to be drawn from an attitude of strict neutrality.

The first and the greatest event of the period was the War of Italian Independence. The French Emperor first helped the Italians, and then deserted them in his own way; but the Italians succeeded in the object of their long endeavours. The first Italian Parliament met in 1861, and Victor Emmanuel assumed the title of the King of Italy. Lord Palmerston sympathized with the Italians, but did not render any active help.

When the Civil War broke out between the Northern and Southern States of America, Lord Palmerston maintained the same neutrality. 'The only thing to do,' he said, 'seems to be to lie on our oars, and to give no pretext to the Washingtonians to quarrel with us, while on the other hand we maintain our rights and those of our fellow-countrymen.'* The war was closed in 1865, and the States remained united.

In 1863 the tyranny of the Russian authorities drove the Poles into insurrection. The action of the Russian Government was described by Lord Napier, the English Ambassador at St. Petersburg, as 'a design to make a clean sweep of the revolutionary youth of Poland.' The sympathy of England for the oppressed Poles, and her disapproval of the policy of Russia, found expression in debate after debate in both Houses of Parliament, and Lord Russell went so far as to lay down six points embodying a perfect amnesty and complete constitutional arrangements. But England would go no farther, and when the French Emperor made a proposal to take action in the matter, Lord Palmerston refused to join. The remonstrance of England was

* 'Viscount Palmerston, K.G.,' by the Marquis of Lorne, K.T. (London, 1892), p. 206.

useless when unsupported by force, and the Polish insurrection was crushed by Russia with cruel and barbarous severity. Men and women were flogged, shot, and hanged, and droves of prisoners, including the flower of the Polish youth, were exiled to Siberia, or perished on the way under the hardships they suffered.

The Danish War excited still greater resentment in England. Bismarck demanded the annexation of Schleswig-Holstein to Germany. England sympathized with Denmark, and the recent marriage of the Prince of Wales with a Danish Princess had drawn closer the relations between the two countries. A conference was held in London in 1864, but did little good. The French Emperor, who had been hurt by England's refusal to join him in support of Poland, now refused to join England in support of Denmark. There was absolutely nothing for it but to leave the Danes alone. 'We abstained,' explained Lord Palmerston, 'in taking the field in defence of Denmark for many reasons—from the season of the year, from the smallness of our army, and the great risk of a failure in a struggle with all Germany by land.'* Denmark, unsupported, fought and was beaten, and the duchies were ceded to Prussia and Austria.

The non-intervention of England in the cause of Denmark aroused bitter feelings among a section of the

* 'Viscount Palmerston, K.G.,' by the Marquis of Lorne, K.T. (London, 1892), p. 211.

English people, specially as England had been prosecuting her little wars in the East. There was a third Chinese war in 1859 and 1860, by which England obtained a favourable treaty. There was a Japanese war in 1862, and Japanese ports were opened to trade. And there was an Ashantee war in 1864, which was not skilfully managed, and English troops fell a prey in large numbers to the pestilential climate. Mr. Disraeli attacked the Government on the Danish question, and urged that 'the course pursued by Government has failed to maintain their avowed policy of upholding the independence and integrity of Denmark, and has lowered the just influence of the country in the capitals of Europe.' And Sir John Hay attacked the Government in reference to the unskilful management of the Ashantee War, and exclaimed that 'the responsibility lies on the Cabinet, the men who had betrayed Denmark and truckled to Germany, who had convulsed China and devastated Japan.'

Such were the bitter charges which were brought against the veteran statesman, whose long career was now drawing to a close. In October, 1865, Lord Palmerston died at the ripe age of eighty-one. He had entered Parliament in 1807, and had been Secretary at War when England was fighting with the great Bonaparte. He was Foreign Secretary when the Reform Bill was passed and when the Queen ascended the throne. He was Home Secretary when the Crimean War broke out, and he concluded that war as Prime Minister.

And he remained the Prime Minister of England from 1855 to his death in 1865, barring a short interval of one year. It may truly be said of him that he had more influence in shaping the foreign policy of England in Europe and in the East, during the lifetime of nearly two generations, than any other man in England. And Englishmen were proud of him, and of his never-failing zeal in upholding the interests and the influence of England throughout the world.

CHAPTER IV.

THE AGE OF DISRAELI AND GLADSTONE.

1865—1885.

THE cry for reform was heard once more in England. As early as 1852, Lord John Russell had attempted a further extension of the suffrage by a Reform Bill, but he was turned out of office before it proceeded further. A second Reform Bill had been introduced by him in 1854, but was withdrawn on the outbreak of the Crimean War. Mr. Disraeli had then framed a Reform Bill under Lord Derby's Government in 1859, but the Bill contained little of real reform, and it failed.

Lord Russell had again introduced a fresh Reform Bill under Palmerston's Government in 1860; but Lord Palmerston himself was lukewarm or hostile, and the Bill had to be withdrawn. It was then felt that there would be no more talk about reforms as long as Lord Palmerston lived. The amusing story is often repeated, that when Lord Palmerston was asked by his butcher why he and his colleagues did not bring in a new Reform Bill, the Prime Minister answered,

'Because we are not geese!' Ardent reformers chafed under the controlling influence of the cynical old statesman. Bishop Wilberforce wrote in 1863: 'That wretched Pam seems to me to get worse and worse. There is not a particle of veracity or noble feeling that I have ever been able to trace in him. He manages the House of Commons by debauching it, making all parties laugh at one another.' But, nevertheless, the large class of Palmerston's admirers liked the veteran statesman, who mocked at enthusiasm, who keenly supported England's interests abroad, and who jocosely burked all efforts for reform at home. There was one earnest man especially who was bent on reform, and whom Palmerston looked upon with some distrust. Once he said to Lord Shaftesbury: 'Gladstone will soon have it all his own way; and, whenever he gets my place, we shall have some strange doings.'

Lord Palmerston died in 1865, and then Mr. Gladstone had it 'all his own way.' Lord John Russell, the aged statesman who had spent half his life in endeavours after reforms, now became Prime Minister, and Mr. Gladstone introduced his Reform Bill in March, 1866. Once more the Reform Bill was ill received. Conservatives and Moderate Liberals combined against it, and formed, in Mr. Bright's words, the Cave of Adullam, into which was invited everyone who was in distress and everyone who was discontented.

The Cave increased in strength, and Mr. Gladstone saw there was little hope of the Bill being passed. This roused him to the utmost, and in winding up the debate on the second reading, on April 28, Mr. Gladstone made one of those great speeches which mark epochs in the history of the British Parliament. Foreseeing the fate of his Bill, he concluded his impassioned speech with words which have become memorable for all age:

'Time is on our side. The great social forces which move onwards in their might and majesty, and which the tumult of our debates does not for a moment impede or disturb—those great social forces are against you; they are marshalled on our side; and the banner which we now carry in this fight, though perhaps at some moment it may droop over our sinking heads, yet it soon again will float in the eye of Heaven, and it will be borne by the firm hands of the united people of the three kingdoms, perhaps not to an easy, but to a certain, and to a not far distant, victory.'

The speech had its effect, and the second reading was carried by a majority of five. This showed, however, that the ultimate fate of the Bill was sealed; and the Government was defeated shortly after, and resigned. The scenes of 1832 were then repeated. Ten thousand people assembled in Trafalgar Square, and voted for reform. Great meetings were held in the large towns of the Northern and Midland counties, and pressed for reform. Gladstone's name was received everywhere with tumultuous acclamation. He had become the popular hero of the day; he was hailed as the leader of the progressive party.

The demands of the people were not made in vain. Lord Derby formed a new Ministry, and Mr. Disraeli introduced a Reform Bill. The more ardent Conservatives were grieved, and Lord Cranborne (afterwards Lord Salisbury) resigned his place as Indian Secretary, and attacked Mr. Disraeli in the *Quarterly Review*. But Mr. Disraeli was helpless: the Conservatives could not hold together without granting a reform, and a reform such as Mr. Gladstone wanted. Mr. Disraeli's Bill was modified in all important points at the dictation of Mr. Gladstone, and when the Bill went up to the House of Lords the Duke of Buccleuch humorously remarked that the only word of the original Bill which remained unaltered was the first word, 'WHEREAS.' The Bill was passed in August, 1867,* and Mr. Disraeli prided himself that he had 'dished the Whigs.'

On the continent of Europe a great event had taken place in 1866. Bismarck steadily pursued his policy to unite Germany under the leadership of Prussia, and the war with Austria which broke out in 1866 promoted the object he had in view. A peace was concluded after the great battle of Sadowa, the existing German Bund was dissolved, and Austria withdrew from the new arrangements of Germany. A Northern and a Southern German confederacy were formed; and Prussia, incorporating Hanover and other northern States in her

* The Bill granted household suffrage in the boroughs, and a £12 franchise in the counties.

dominions, became the leader of the Northern Confederacy. England maintained a policy of neutrality as before. She had a little war of her own in Abyssinia, which was brought to a satisfactory conclusion by Napier at Magdala in 1867. The cost of the war was enormous, and a part of it was debited to India, under the plea that the necessity of the war had arisen chiefly from the effect which the impunity of the King of Abyssinia would have upon the Eastern mind, and therefore on the interests of the Indian Empire! The debiting of the cost of an African war to India was bad; the argument used to justify it was worse.

Lord John Russell's task was done when the Reform Bill of 1867 was passed, and the aged statesman, now in his seventy-sixth year, retired from politics. In the following February Lord Derby resigned his Premiership on account of his failing health. The ancient leaders of Parliament thus retired from the scene one by one, and left the field open to those who have been the leaders of our generation. It is remarkable that while we had six Prime Ministers during the first thirty years of the Queen's reign—Melbourne, Peel, Russell, Derby, Aberdeen, and Palmerston—we have only had four Prime Ministers during the next thirty years of her reign—Disraeli, Gladstone, Salisbury, and Rosebery.

Lord Derby's resignation was accepted in February, 1868, and Mr. Disraeli was appointed Prime Minister. His tenure of office on this occasion was, however, short.

The question of the Irish Church came up for discussion, and Mr. Gladstone introduced three resolutions, declaring that, in the opinion of the House, the Irish Church should cease to exist. The Government was defeated in the debates, and at the new elections, which took place in the latter end of the year, the Liberals had a majority of over a hundred. The Conservative Ministry resigned, and Mr. Gladstone became Prime Minister in December, 1868. The Duke of Argyll became the Indian Secretary; John Bright was President of the Board of Trade; Mr. Lowe and Mr. Goschen, and Lords Hartington and Ripon, Dufferin and Kimberley were in the Cabinet.

The history of the next five years is a history of great reforms. A strong Liberal spirit inspired the Ministry and the nation alike, and Liberal measures were passed in quick succession. On March 1, 1869, Mr. Gladstone introduced his momentous Bill for the disestablishment of the Irish Church in a great speech of three hours, and Mr. Bright supported it in a speech of infinite beauty and pathos. The second reading was carried by a majority of over a hundred, and the Bill was passed into law in July.

Next came Mr. Gladstone's Bill to reform the Irish land laws. The crying need for the reform had been felt for over a quarter of a century, but the influence of landlords was great, and had hitherto obstructed legislation. Half measures, worse than no measures, had been adopted to relieve the distressed Irish tenant, but legislators had shrunk from bestowing on him any sort of tenant-right. 'Tenant-right was landlord's wrong,' Lord Palmerston had said, in his bantering manner, and this sorry jest was considered as the final word on the controversy. But a statesman of a different stamp had now undertaken to redress the wrongs of the Irish tenants. Mr. Gladstone's object was to protect the tenant from eviction as long as he paid his rent, and to secure to him the value of improvements which his industry had made; and the proposed protection was therefore not unlike that which Lord Canning had bestowed on Bengal tenants over ten years before. The Bill was introduced in February, 1870, and was passed in the same year.

In the same year was introduced the great measure for a national and compulsory system of elementary education. Mr. Forster's Bill met with great opposition, and there was prolonged discussion as to details, but the English nation had made up their minds on the subject. The Bill was at last passed, providing school accommodation for all the children in England, and exerting pressure on parents to fulfil their duty in training their children. The beneficent results of this great measure are obvious after the lapse of a quarter of a century. Foreigners who were in England before 1870, and who are revisiting the country now, find a striking and remarkable change for the better, not only in the general conduct and manners, but also in the habits of prudence and foresight and in the moral behaviour, of the lower classes in England.*

Other reforms followed in the succeeding years. The long-vexed question of religious tests at the Universities was settled; the abolition of purchase in the army was decreed; the army was reorganized and the country was divided into districts with central depôts for the home battalions; and the Civil Service was thrown open to public competition. But the country was becoming tired of the Liberal Government. Forster's Ballot Bill was thrown out by the Lords in 1871, but was passed in the following year; Mr. Goschen's Bill for the reform of local government and taxation was thrown out; Mr. Lowe's proposed tax on matches, introduced with the punning motto, *Ex luce lucellum*, was opposed and thrown out. The foreign policy of the Government was also strongly criticised.

The great Franco-Prussian War broke out in 1870. The French Emperor, who had come to be regarded with distrust by all European Powers, was hurled from his throne. The Empire was abolished, and a French Republic was proclaimed. The King of Prussia assumed the title of Emperor of Germany, and all German States were to some extent united under him. Two French

* The present writer had the good fortune to be in England in the stirring years 1868, 1869 and 1870; and nothing has impressed him more, in re-visiting England in the nineties, than the remarkable change in the lower classes. The worst signs of degradation which one noticed in the lowest classes thirty years ago seem to have altogether disappeared.

provinces were wrested from France, and added to Germany. England had remained neutral during the war, and her conduct was sharply criticised.

Russia threw off the restrictions imposed upon her after the Crimean War by neutralizing the Black Sea, and England could take no action to prevent this. America demanded compensation for loss inflicted on her by privateers fitted out in England; the *Alabama* claims were submitted to arbitration, and the verdict went against England. All these events lowered the popularity of the Government, although its action in each of these cases was strictly correct. Finally, a fresh Ashantee War broke out in 1873, and it was after immense difficulty brought to a successful conclusion by Sir Garnet Wolseley. But Gladstone's ministry had fallen in the meantime. The Parliament had been dissolved, the Conservatives had a majority of fifty after the new elections, and Mr. Disraeli became Prime Minister in 1874.

The first administration of Mr. Gladstone, which closed in 1874, was contemporaneous with the rule, in India, of two of the ablest and best Viceroys who have ever gone out to that dependency since it passed under the direct rule of the Crown. Lord Mayo, who succeeded Sir John Lawrence in 1869, was an Irish nobleman, remarkably well fitted for the post of an Indian Viceroy. Noble and courtly in his demeanour, genial and affable in his manners, he won a larger share of personal love and respect than ordinarily falls to the lot of Governor-Generals in India. His strong common-sense and generous instincts were a safer guide in the complications of Indian administration than a mere knowledge of details acquired by long residence in India, and his indefatigable industry in the cause of the welfare of the people whose concerns he administered enabled him to effect improvement in various departments. The immense extension of roads, railways, and canals which took place under his administration greatly developed the resources of the country, while his provincial decentralization scheme infused fresh life into the administration of the different Provinces. It is sad to contemplate that an assassin's knife terminated his noble and useful career at Port Blair in 1872.

He was succeeded by Lord Northbrook, an administrator of Liberal principles and strong practical sense, which left its impress on his Indian administration. A famine broke out in Behar in 1874, and to Lord Northbrook belongs the credit of having, for the first time in the history of British India, succeeded completely in relieving distress and preventing deaths in an Indian famine. After the famine was over, the Prince of Wales visited India in 1875-76, and the outburst of loyalty which the visit evoked from all sections of the people in all parts of India forms one of the most memorable events of modern Indian history.

Mr. Disraeli had become Prime Minister in 1874,

and a change came over the spirit of England's policy towards Afghanistan. The policy of maintaining that country as a strong, independent but friendly State had been accepted by successive Viceroys—Lawrence, Mayo, and Northbrook—and had been consistently acted upon. But a new policy was now mooted, viz., that English agents should be established in the heart of Afghanistan in order to control that power more effectually. Lord Salisbury, now Secretary of State for India, sent a despatch embodying the new policy in January, 1875. Lord Northbrook, strong in the strength of his own convictions, remonstrated. In the following year he again differed from the Secretary of State on the financial policy of India. He received a censure, and resigned.

Lord Lytton was then sent out to India, entrusted with the duty of giving effect to the new policy towards Afghanistan. He had instructions to find an excuse for sending a mission to Kabul, and for insisting on the keeping of an English resident in Afghanistan. The mistake which previous Governor-Generals had guarded against was now committed.

The first great act of Lord Lytton in India was, however, auspicious, and called forth an outburst of loyalty from the Indian people. On January 1, 1877, Lord Lytton proclaimed to the princes and people of India that the Queen of England had assumed the august title of the Empress of India. This was announced to an imperial assemblage in the historic town of Delhi, and it was also announced in similar meetings in every district town in India. But while the great message was thus notified amidst circumstances of pomp and splendour, the shadow of a great famine was already darkening over Southern India. Crops had failed through want of seasonable rain, and the measures taken to relieve the people were inadequate. The disaster grew to be the most terrible and fatal which has ever visited India within this century, and *five millions* of the population of India died from starvation, or from diseases caused by insufficient nourishment. The destruction of life from the most calamitous and prolonged wars pales before this great and terrible disaster, the like of which has not been known in the modern history of any other country or nation.

In the following year Lord Lytton declared war against Kabul. He had tried to gain his object by negotiations, and had failed; and to his demand that an English representative should be received in Afghanistan the ruler of that country had replied by a request for the relaxation of that condition. In the meantime, the Amir had received a Russian mission, and an English mission with an escort of over 1,000 men had been refused. The result was war. The Prime Minister of England, now Lord Beaconsfield, disclosed that the true object of the war was to form a 'scientific frontier.'

The British army was completely successful, and the Amir fled, only to die. His son, Yakub Khan, presented himself at the British camp, and signed the Treaty of Gundamuck in May, 1879. The Indian Government agreed to pay the Amir £60,000 a year, and the Amir ceded the 'scientific frontier,' and agreed to allow a British representative to reside in Kabul. The treaty gave rise, as on a previous occasion, to a false sense of security, and a British resident was sent to reside in Kabul.

In September the terrible news was received that the British resident with his escort had been murdered. A fresh invasion of Kabul took place in October, and a new Amir, Abdur Rahman, was placed on the throne. In 1880 the Conservative Government was overthrown in England, and Lord Lytton resigned his post in India, and was succeeded by Lord Ripon. A defeat of the British army at Maiwand was promptly retrieved by General Roberts by a splendid victory, and as soon as matters were a little settled the English withdrew from Afghanistan.

The enormous cost of this Afghan war has been succeeded by a steady increase in the cost of the Indian army, mainly owing to the extension of the Indian frontier. The requirements of the imperial policy of England with reference to Russia have also caused an increase in the strength of the Indian army, so as to allow of a powerful field army being placed beyond the Indian frontier, in addition to the army required to keep internal peace in India. It is neither equitable nor possible for India to meet all this additional expenditure.

The extreme poverty of the people of India is becoming patent every day, and the administration of the country is now virtually starved to meet the growing imperial expenditure. The developments which have taken place in the frontier policy of India, during the last twenty years, under the direction of Her Majesty's Government in England, render it imperative that England should bear a portion of the cost of maintaining her Asiatic empire. The proposal has been made by high authorities, and is both equitable and unavoidable, and we will revert to it further on.

While the Afghan war was going on in the East, Europe was the scene of a sanguinary war. An insurrection in Bulgaria had been repressed by Turkey with barbarous cruelty, which made all Europe indignant. Mr. Gladstone, who had retired from politics some time before, appeared once more upon the scene, and roused the indignation of the English nation by impassioned speeches, which were, perhaps, the most powerful that even he ever made. Russia undertook, single-handed, the redress of the oppressed Christians in Turkey, and declared war in 1877. The Turks made a gallant resistance, but the Russians eventually triumphed, and forced Turkey to conclude the Treaty of San Stefano in March, 1878.

The jealousy of Russia had not died out in England. A British fleet appeared in the Sea of Marmora, and 7,000 Indian troops were summoned to Malta. The Treaty of San Stefano was submitted for the consideration of the Powers at the Berlin Congress, and the Berlin Treaty was signed in July, 1878. North Bulgaria obtained its independence and South Bulgaria obtained a sort of self-government; Servia and Montenegro were freed; Bosnia and Herzgovina were placed under Austria; Batoum and Kars were left to Russia; Greece obtained an improved frontier; and England obtained the island of Cyprus. The 'integrity of Turkey,' thus mutilated, was once more preserved.

In the meantime, complications had arisen in South Africa, and the Transvaal was annexed to the British dominions in 1877. A war with the Zulus followed in the next year, and a British force was destroyed by the Zulus at Isandlana early in 1879. The disaster was retrieved, and the country of the Zulus was divided among the leading native chiefs.

The course of events in Bulgaria, in Afghanistan, and in Zululand had greatly impaired the popularity of Lord Beaconsfield's Government. Mr. Gladstone's famous 'Midlothian Campaign' of 1879 had also shaken the Government, and when the Parliament was dissolved in 1880, Mr. Gladstone went forth on his second 'Midlothian Campaign.' 'The walls of the Tory Jericho of the North went down before the blast of his trumpet;' the son of the Duke of Buccleuch, then the most notable Scottish peer, was defeated on his own ground; the Tory party was routed in the North, and only nine Conservatives were returned from Scotland. The Liberals were returned to Parliament in an overwhelming majority over the Conservatives and the Irish Home Rulers combined. The Queen sent for Lord Hartington. Lord Hartington and Lord Granville explained to Her Majesty that the victory was Mr. Gladstone's, and that the Liberal party would be satisfied with no other leader. The same evening Mr. Gladstone kissed hands, and became Prime Minister of England for the second time.

Ireland again claimed the attention of Mr. Gladstone. A succession of bad harvests had caused much suffering and discontent among the tenants. A Land League was formed which advised tenants not to pay rents, and acts of violence were perpetrated. Mr. Gladstone went, as before, to the root of the matter. The Government carried a Land Act in 1881, granting what is called the three F's to tenants—fair rents, fixity of tenure, and freedom of sale. The Land League was then forcibly suppressed, and after the murder of Lord Cavendish and Mr. Burke in Dublin, a strong Crimes Act was passed and firmly administered. The country was quiet for the next two years.

But the Liberal administration was greatly impeded by the entanglements of foreign wars which were forced on Mr. Gladstone. The Boers of the Transvaal chafed under the British Government, and rose in rebellion in 1881. The British force was defeated at Laing's Nek and at Majuba Hill, and the Boers secured a sort of independence under the suzerainty of England.

In Egypt Arabi Pasha inaugurated the policy of

'Egypt for the Egyptians,' and fortified Alexandria and massed troops. England interfered, against the wishes of many of the prominent Liberals, and Mr. Bright resigned his office rather than be a party to a policy of war. Admiral Seymour bombarded the forts of Alexandria, and at Tel-el-Kebir Sir Garnet Wolseley crushed Arabi Pasha, who was banished to Ceylon. The power of the Khedive was restored, but the British have, since then, continued to occupy Egypt.

The Egyptian policy of England led to fresh complications. The tribes in the Soudan rose under the 'Mahdi,' and a British force was surrounded and annihilated. The famous Gordon was sent to settle matters. He reached Khartoum in February, 1884, defended the town against the besiegers for one year with extraordinary energy and resource, and vainly asked for succour. In January, 1885, Khartoum fell with its heroic defender.

The Liberal Government was now doomed, but it succeeded in passing one great measure before it laid down its power. The great Reform Act of 1832 had taken away the political power in the country from the peers and a limited number of influential families, and had vested it in the great middle classes. The Reform Act of 1867 had extended the suffrage, and had given the working-classes a share in the administration. But it had left a distinction between the boroughs and the counties, and virtually the working-classes in the boroughs were allowed a franchise from which the working-classes in the counties were excluded. The defect was remedied, and the system of representation was made complete by the third Reform Act, which placed the voters in the counties and those in the boroughs on the same footing. The Lords at first threw out the Bill on the ground that it made no provision for the redistribution of seats. A redistribution scheme had, therefore, to be introduced, and Mr. Gladstone agreed with Lord Salisbury as to its details. The Reform Act was passed in December, 1884, and the Redistribution Act in the following year. Mr. Gladstone resigned in June, 1885, and Lord Salisbury became Prime Minister.

It remains now only to say one or two words about India during Mr. Gladstone's second administration. Lord Ripon had gone out to India with a desire to govern the country on Liberal lines, and his administration was far-sighted and wise. We have seen before that he withdrew British troops from Kabul after the affairs in that country had been settled to some extent. He repealed the fetters which his predecessor had placed on the vernacular press of India; and he showed his trust and confidence in the people of India by introducing a scheme of local self-government. The experience and local knowledge of the people are of great value in the administration of local affairs in every Indian district, and Lord Ripon's measure secured this to a somewhat larger extent than had been done before, and thus gave a somewhat wider scope to

Indians in the management of their own concerns. The Municipal Act was also recast, the election of the members by the rate-payers was provided for, and the members were permitted to elect their own chairman.

Lord Canning had granted a substantial protection to the cultivators of Bengal in 1859. The Act of 1859 was revised in 1868, but it had become now necessary to extend its provisions by a fresh Act. Lord Ripon instituted inquiries in every district, and thus obtained a valuable mass of facts and opinions from men who were familiar with details, and were competent to speak on the subject. On these valuable materials he framed a Tenancy Act, which was passed, with some modification, by his successor, Lord Dufferin, in 1885. Throughout the period of his administration, Lord Ripon worked with a single-hearted desire to benefit the people placed under him; and his endeavours were crowned with success, firstly in some extension of powers to the educated people of India, and secondly in the ample protection given to the uneducated cultivators.

Lord Ripon left India in 1884, amidst manifestations of the people's love and loyalty such as have been seldom witnessed in India. And an imaginative and grateful Hindu poet, who sings of India reviving under the British Rule, records in feeling verse:

> 'That form, yet fair, with tremor shakes,
> As slowly she responsive wakes
> At Bentinck's, Canning's, Ripon's call!'

We close our story here, as the events of the last twelve years are too fresh for a historical review. It has often been said, and said correctly, that India has been conquered, not by the sword, but by good government, and that she is retained, not by the sword, but by good government. The sword is required to repress occasional local disturbances among hill tribes, or to keep out foreign invaders; but the sword did not conquer the people, and could not keep the people for a single generation without good government. The people of India, although extremely pacific, are a power, and that power was drawn to the support of the British rule from the very commencement by good government. In the days of anarchy which succeeded the Mogul rule in India, the people of India were drawn spontaneously to the rule which gave them security and peace, and which, in spite of many blunders, is honest in its purpose, and beneficent in its work. The leading men in Bengal welcomed the British power in the days of Clive and Hastings; the village communities of Northern India hailed the triumphs of the Marquis of Wellesley; and the harassed peasantry of Madras and Bombay supported the British power in the days of Munro and Elphinstone.

The history of British conquests is the history of popular support, which has never wavered in the cause of a civilized administration. And this popular support witnessed no change and no decadence, even when mutinous sepoys rose in thousands in the dark days of

1857, and threatened to engulf the British power in ruin.

Within the forty years which have since elapsed, there have been no great wars within the limits of India, and in as far as it is permitted to us to anticipate the future, there will be no wars so long as the people are held together by a wise and a progressive government. The strongest support of the British rule in India is an enlightened administration which draws towards it the sympathy and the co-operation of the people. The strongest tie which links India to England is the tie of a beneficent and progressive rule. These words have often been said, but those who know India well, those who have passed their lifetime in the work of administration among the people of India, know that these words are not vain platitudes. Indian districts contain vast populations, managed by a handful of officials. We ourselves have been in charge of many a district in India, with a population of two or three millions, with no troops within a hundred miles of the district, and with a Civil Police numbering less than 500. The real strength of the position of a district officer and his ten or twelve subordinate executive officers, under such circumstances, is the support rendered by the two or three million villagers themselves—rendered without question or hesitation, because they feel confidence in the justice, the good faith, the honesty of the rule which the handful of officials represent. Without this silent but effective support, the

British army were vain against a population like that of India; and with this support, which can always be secured by a wise and progressive administration, the British army has scarcely any work in the settled districts of India.

Much has been written of late against the Indian press, and the agitation of the people. But the worst criticisms of the press are criticisms, not against the British rule, but against the errors of administration, against blundering methods and faulty procedure. And the most influential agitation of the people is an agitation, not against the British government, but with a view to improve the administration, to bring it more in touch with the people, and to make it less liable to the mistakes incident to a foreign rule. To these matters we will recur in the next chapter.

CHAPTER V.

CONCLUSION.

THE object which we placed before ourselves in undertaking this little work was to show that the administration of India is determined by the current of opinions in England, that progress in India is stimulated by English progress, and that the history of India under British rule is shaped by those great influences which make for reforms in Europe. This is a fact which is often overlooked by the historians of India, but Indian history is unintelligible to us without this explanation. From the time of the great Pitt to the time of Mr. Gladstone, English influences have inspired the rulers of India; English history and Indian history have run in parallel streams. The reforms and wars of Pitt in Europe had their influence on the reforms of Cornwallis and the wars of Wellesley; and popular progress in England under Canning and Grey led to the extension of privileges granted to the people of India by Munro, Elphinstone, and Bentinck. The able and vigorous, if somewhat hectoring, policy of Palmerston was reflected in the vigorous but ill-judged acts of Auckland and Dalhousie; and Mr. Gladstone's Liberal measures during his first and second administrations were reflected in the Liberal administrations of Mayo, Northbrook and Ripon. India has advanced with England, has occasionally blundered with England, but has in the long run moved onwards, however slowly, in the path of progress chalked out by England.

To the people of India this is a great consolation. We feel assured by the knowledge that we have thrown in our lot with a nation, not only one of the greatest on earth, but also one of the most progressive. We feel assured by the belief that, under the wise dispensations of Providence, the progress of England is our progress, England's gain our gain. And we feel assured by the idea, which is as true as it is encouraging, that every generation of English statesmen necessarily exert their influence on Indian administration, that their endeavours stimulate our progress, their successes lead to our reforms.

It is necessary to remember these facts, to repeat them and to emphasize them, because they serve to dispel many illusions. They dispel the illusions of forlorn and faint-hearted pessimists, who can see no progress in India, because we are not moving at the rate they would prescribe, and in the lines they would lay down. But if we are correct in our narration and estimate of facts in the preceding chapters, surely the history of India during a hundred years has been emphatically a history of progress. In the greater protection now afforded to life and property, in the spread of education and culture, and in the extension of popular rights and privileges, we have moved onwards, and we expect to move onwards still, as long as our fortunes are linked with the fortunes of England. The times are with us, and the signs of the times are so clear that he who runs may read.

On the other hand, there is a class of extreme and unreasoning optimists who are so well satisfied with the present condition of India that they desire no progress in the future. All criticism, however moderate, annoys them by disturbing their roseate view of things, and every proposal of reform fills them with alarm. Thoughtful Indians, who suggest improvements in the present methods of administration, are pronounced by them to be discontented and disloyal; and political bodies in India, which express the wishes and aspirations of the people, are branded by them as seditious.

Unreasoning optimism makes a mistake here. Rightly viewed, the influential political bodies in India are the strongest supports of the British rule. Those bodies consist of the leaders of the Indian communities, educated, intelligent, loyal by their own interests, interpreters between the rulers and the people, men who have everything to gain by the continuance of the British rule, men who have staked everything on that rule, men who have everything to lose by the severance of India from

England. Their view of things is not always the official view; and it is a gain, therefore, when the official view is so constantly and prominently placed before the public, that the non-official view should also find some expression. Their criticism is not always pleasant to officials; but public criticism is always beneficial to the cause of good government, and it is a notable fact that the administration is purest in those parts of India where public criticism is the strongest. They do not speak with the knowledge of details which officials can justly lay claim to; but their general views and opinions are not necessarily wrong, and it is a gain to know what the views of the leaders of the people are. It would be a wise policy, therefore, to treat the influential political bodies in India with courtesy and respect even when their suggestions cannot be accepted; it would be an unwise policy to repress or discredit them in the eyes of the nation. To discredit or repress them would be to allow opportunities to wilder spirits, who are kept down by the influence of the educated classes. It would be exchanging criticism which we hear, and methods of work which we see, for less educated and less legitimate criticism which we shall not hear, and darker methods of work which we shall not see. The worst enemies of England could not devise a policy more disastrous to her interests; and sections of English politicians and of the English press, which are seeking to discredit and repress the movements of the educated, loyal, and intelligent communities of India, are playing into the hands of England's enemies, and are creating difficulties for the British rule in India.

We have spoken of forlorn pessimists who can see no progress in the past, and of unreasoning optimists who desire no reforms in the future. Between these extreme sections it is possible to take our stand on the safe ground of rational optimism. Our readers who have accompanied us through the preceding pages will have seen that, while narrating, as clearly and emphatically as we could, the progress that has been made by the Indian administration, we have not hesitated to indicate its mistakes and point out its blunders. And while we have taken pains to describe fully the reforms which have been effected in the past, we have not shrunk from hinting at the legacy of difficulties which has been left to us, and which we shall have to face in the future. To describe those difficulties fully, and to explain their remedies clearly, would require a separate work; but nevertheless our review of the past administration of India were vain if it did not point to some obvious reforms needed in the future.

The gravest difficulty which English administrators have to face in India lies in the extreme poverty of the Indian population. Four-fifths of the population of India depend upon agriculture, and administrators who have passed their lifetime among the Indian cultivators are aware of their state of almost hopeless poverty and indebtedness. Except in Bengal, where the condition of the cultivator is secured by the Permanent Settlement and by sound land laws, the Indian cultivator is generally in the hands of the money-lender, never saving or hoping to save, paying his rent and his interest after the annual harvest if it is a good one, and getting into debt immediately after. It is estimated from official records that one-fifth of the Indian rural population, or between 40,000,000 and 50,000,000 of people, are insufficiently fed even in years of good harvest. The other four-fifths are tolerably well off in good years, but if the rains hold off for a single year and the crops fail, they are without help or resource, and they depend upon their paddy lenders, or on their landlords, or on the State for help. The stores of paddy in the country, as has been proved by inquiries in the present year of famine, are insignificant, and the mass of the agricultural population live year after year on the year's produce. And their poverty, their chronic indebtedness, and their want of resource, form one of the gravest problems which we have to face.

There have been no serious wars within the geographical limits of India during forty years; cultivation has extended as rapidly as the population of the country; communications by rail and steamer have been opened; and all the causes which in other lands conduce to the prosperity of a nation have been in operation. Nevertheless, it is a fact that the people of India, outside the permanently settled provinces, are in hopeless poverty, and every year of a bad harvest is a year of scarcity or of famine. Five times within this peaceful period of forty years, large areas of the country were desolated by that terrible calamity. In 1860 and in 1866 the loss of life was terrible; in 1874 it was prevented by the noble and determined endeavours of Lord Northbrook; in 1877 the operations of relief broke down, and five millions of the people were swept away from Southern India; and in the present year, in spite of the excellent arrangements made for the relief of sufferers, the death rate has been high in the famine-stricken provinces. It is sad to contemplate this state of the population of India after over a hundred years of British rule, and after forty years of profound internal peace. If there be a cause for this state of things, it must be found out; if there be a remedy for this, it must be applied.

At such a crisis as this any unseasonable optimism, which conceals from us the real poverty of the Indian people, is hurtful to the interests both of England and of India. Figures often mislead us unless rightly explained. We have been told that the trade of India has increased by leaps and bounds, and the increase in trade must mean the prosperity of the people. We have been told that the total value of India's exports and imports has increased from Rs. 20,000,000 to over Rs. 200,000,000 within the present reign. The export of tea from India has risen from nothing to 150,000,000 pounds; the export of cotton has increased from nothing to 11,000,000 hundredweight; the production of jute has increased from almost nothing to 1,000,000 tons; the export of wheat has risen from nothing to 750,000 tons; coal is produced every year to the extent of 3,000,000 tons, and there is increase in the production or export of various other articles which form articles of trade. Twenty thousand miles of railway have been constructed, and steamers ply in all the navigable rivers of India.

We have no desire to minimize the prosperity of the English trade with India which these figures indicate; but when they are brought forward to prove that the material condition of the industrial and agricultural population of India has improved, a great fallacy is committed. Among the many blessings which England has conferred on India, the encouragement of Indian industries is not one. The increase in the value of imports into India really means that the manual industries of India have died out in an unequal competition with the steam and machinery of England. And the increase in the value of exports from India means that vast quantities of food and raw material have to be sent out from India to pay for imported English goods. In the early days of the Company's rule, fabrics produced by Indian weavers supplied the markets of Europe, and men still living can remember the days when every village in the weaving districts had its looms, and millions of Indian weavers were supported by that profitable industry. How this industry was gradually strangled and destroyed, first by protective duties imposed on Indian goods in England,* and then by an unequal competition; how Indian weavers who were content with threepence or fourpence a day found themselves ruined by the cheaper products of English looms; and how the weaver communities of India were compelled to abandon their trade, and to depend on agriculture or petty trade, or on humble and ill-paid appointments in public or private offices—all this forms one of the saddest chapters in the history of British India. What happened to the weavers has also happened to the other industrial classes. The production of lac

* 'It is also a melancholy instance of the wrong done to India by the country on which she has become dependent. It was stated in evidence (1813) that the cotton and silk goods of India up to the period could be sold for a profit in the British market at a price from 50 to 60 per cent. lower than those fabricated in England. It consequently became necessary to protect the latter by duties of 70 and 80 per cent. on their value, or by positive prohibition. Had this not been the case, had not such prohibitory duties and decrees existed, the mills of Paisley and Manchester would have been stopped in their outset, and could scarcely have been again set in motion, even by the power of steam. They were created by the sacrifice of the Indian manufacture. Had India been independent, she would have retaliated; would have imposed preventive duties upon British goods, and would thus have preserved her own productive industry from annihilation. This act of self-defence was not permitted her; she was at the mercy of the stranger. British goods were forced upon her without paying any duty, and the foreign manufacturer employed the arm of political injustice to keep down and ultimately strangle a competitor with whom he could not have contended on equal terms.'—Mill and Wilson's 'History of British India' (London, 1858), vol. vii., p. 385.

dyes has died out since the importation of aniline dyes, and Indian workers in metals and in leather can scarcely hold their own against imported goods. Millions of artisans have been ousted from their occupations, and have taken to agriculture, and the pressure on the resources of the soil has thus increased with the decadence of our industries. We have ourselves seen, and all Indian administrators who have spent years of their life in the old weaving districts have seen, that the old villages of weavers are often overgrown with jungle, temples constructed by those classes are in decay, large irrigation tanks excavated by them are silted up, and have not been redug or replaced by other tanks. The villages know not their artisan population who flourished there of old; they have dispersed all over the country as agriculturists, or have crowded to towns as petty traders. 'Leave off weaving; supply us with the raw material, and we will weave for you,' was virtually what the East India Company said to the Indian weaver at the beginning of the century,* and this mandate has been only too scrupulously and cruelly followed.

Cotton and jute are grown in India in fields which produced or would have produced rice or wheat. Nearly one-half of the large eastern district of Maimansingh, about 6,000 square miles in area, produces jute instead of rice, and many other Bengal

* Mill and Wilson's 'History of British India,' vol. vii., p. 385.

districts produce the same fibre in smaller quantities. Cotton is grown over large areas all over India, where rice or wheat might have been grown. The production of these fibres on a large scale in India supplies the manufactories of Great Britain with materials for their looms. At the same time the extension of cotton and jute cultivation in India shows that it must be more profitable than rice or wheat in the areas in which they are grown. The profit remains in the country, with the cultivators, where the State demand from the soil has been permanently limited; but over the larger portion of India the recurring settlements, securing a steady increase in the State demand, sweep away the increased profits to the imperial exchequer, and leave the tillers of the soil no better off than before.

Railways and carrying steamers in India have been constructed with English capital, and the interest and profit come to England. Nevertheless, these improved means of communication benefit the country in a variety of ways, and not the least beneficent effect is the opening up of markets for surplus produce. Large tracts of the country, the produce of which had scarcely any market in the olden days beyond the local demand, have benefited by these new means of communication, and the prices of the produce have generally risen in India. But in this case also, the increased profit remains with the people where the State demand has been permanently limited. In the greater portion of India it is claimed by the State. Indeed, land revenue settlements are made for short periods in tracts where new lines of railway are under construction, in order that the benefits conferred by the new lines may be secured by the State at the expiration of such short periods.

New products like tea are now grown in India; but they are grown mostly by English companies with English capital. The profit comes to England, and does not benefit the Indian agriculturist. And the special law under which labourers for tea-gardens are recruited has been described as 'slave-law' in India. Women and boys are sometimes seduced or kidnapped to the gardens, and ignorant men are supposed to contract to work for years, and are arrested and punished if they attempt to run away.

Imports of gold on private account, and not for purposes of coinage, have averaged annually more than £2,500,000, and it is fondly imagined that this gold is secretly hoarded by the cultivators of India! Unreasoning optimism does not stop to calculate that, if this gold was shared equally by the population of India, the share of each cultivator would be about *twopence in the year*, the price of one glass of beer in England, the price of one day's rice-meal in India! As a matter of fact, the annual import of gold represents the wear and tear in the gold jewellery and brocades, etc., which are almost the only luxury of the wealthier classes in India. The import of gold into India no more indicates the wealth of the Indian cultivator than the import of silk hats and kid gloves from Paris indicates the wealth of the British farm-labourer.

We have dwelt on these facts, not with the idea of over-colouring a picture which is sufficiently dismal in its true outlines, but in order that we may clearly recognise the hard fact of the extreme poverty of India —a fact which is often obscured by misleading trade figures. Trade and public works, carried on or constructed in a country with its own capital, are evidence of the material prosperity of the people. In the case of India they are profitable investments of English capital, and while they undoubtedly benefit India in a variety of ways, they have not secured the object of materially improving the condition of the agricultural and artisan classes of India.

Well-informed writers, who obtain their information from official records, know this; they admit the extreme poverty of the agricultural classes; and they have recorded the dismal fact that nearly one-fifth of the rural population of India are insufficiently fed, even in ordinary years. But the cause of this poverty is often misunderstood, and it is often attributed to the reckless increase of the population. It can be proved, however, by figures, that though the people of India marry early, they do not increase at a higher rate than the people of many European countries. Within the period of the Queen's reign the population of the British Islands has increased from 25,000,000 to 40,000,000, not counting 10,000,000 more who have found homes beyond the seas. In India, excluding new annexations and conquests, the population has not increased at this rate; nor has it increased out of proportion to the extension of cultivation. In the British Islands the wealth per head of the population has increased from £144 to £302, while the incidence of taxation remains the same;* in other words, the proportion of taxation to wealth has gone down to one half within the Queen's reign. In India we have no figures to show if the wealth per head of the population has increased at all; but the incidence of the taxes derived from the agricultural classes, from land, from salt, and from local cesses, has considerably increased.

Our readers will pardon our dwelling at some length on this subject. No subject which is before the public now affects the well-being of a larger number of human beings and of British subjects; and no subject has a more melancholy interest in this year, when, in the midst of the exuberant prosperity of all parts of the British Empire, India alone sends us a tragic tale of poverty, famine and death. But we have dwelt on this subject, not with the object of raising a discordant note in a year of jubilation, but because it is necessary that we should recognise a hard, undeniable and melancholy fact in order that we may find out its true remedy. Two remedies will suggest themselves to our readers; the first is a protection of Indian industries, the second

* 'National Progress during the Queen's Reign,' by Michael G. Mulhall. (London: Routledge and Sons, 1897.)

is a permanent limitation of the State demand from the soil. The first is probably not within the range of practical politics in these days, and we will say no more about it. The second would be the saving of India.

We have already explained elsewhere this remedy for bettering the condition of the Indian agriculturists. It is a remedy which was adopted in Bengal by Lord Cornwallis in the last century, which has saved the greater part of Bengal from famines, and has secured to the cultivators and landlords the increasing profits from the soil. It is a remedy which was extended to Benares by Lord Teignmouth towards the close of the last century, and which was proposed for all India by Lord Canning after the famine of 1860. The very mention of a permanent settlement of land revenues frightens many modern Indian administrators, but surely the principles of such a settlement could be accepted and applied to the varying circumstances of each Province. That this is a reform urgently needed will scarcely be denied by unbiassed men. So long as fresh revenue settlements are made every thirty, twenty, or even fifteen years, securing an increase in the demand from the soil, it is idle to talk of improvement in the material condition of the people of India. A severe famine is desolating the greater part of India in the present year, but the settlement officer is still at his work. A large increase in the State demand has been obtained from the Central Provinces of India, and a large increase is expected in the Province of Orissa, where settlement operations are now proceeding. It were well if the people of the Central Provinces and of Orissa were assured that this large increase is the last, that henceforward England desires the cultivators of India to reap the increase in the income from the soil. A permanent limitation to the State demand from the soil would be a fitting gift from their gracious Queen-Empress in this year of the Diamond Jubilee to the impoverished people of India.*

* It gives us much pleasure to quote, in support of our view, the following passages from the article on Indian Affairs in *The Times* of April 27, 1897 :

'Among the conditions which make for the permanent prosperity of agricultural races, fixity of tenure holds a foremost place. Throughout almost all India the Government lets the land to the people on thirty years leases, and subject to certain provisions can, and as a matter of fact does, raise the rent at the expiry of each term. It thus secures the unearned increment for the State, and is enabled to provide for currency and other fiscal contingencies by keeping a firm hold on land. But shrewd observers assert that the absence of a permanent settlement operates as a discouragement to improvement, and that as a matter of fact the Government pays dearly for its power to raise the rent by checking the prosperity of the people. . . .

'The time has arrived for the expiry of the thirty years' settlement of 1867, and the Orissa landholders ask the Government to redeem its pledges. They declare that "all the conditions precedent to the fulfilment of the promise of a permanent settlement have now been satisfied"; that "the fullest infor. mation has now been gathered in regard to the points noted in" the law of 1816, and in other legislative Acts, as necessary to enable a permanent settlement to be fairly made ; and that the economic history of the province in the past and its actual necessities in the present alike point to the expediency of the

But it will be asked, If the State demand from the soil be thus limited, how will it be possible to meet the growing expenditure of India? This brings us to the second reform we have to propose: the growing public expenditure of India requires to be checked to some extent. The military expenditure of India, specially, has grown beyond all proportion to the resources of the country; and this has happened in the lifetime of a generation which has lived in profound peace, and has witnessed no serious war within the natural frontiers of India. Every official who has taken a share in the work of Indian administration is aware that the civil administration of the country has been starved to find ways and means for the military expenditure. High and responsible rulers of different Provinces in India have protested in no uncertain voice against a system which takes away, once every five years, an increasing

---

measure. Amid a long series of promises, pledges, and fluctuations of policy, spread over ninety-three years, there are doubtless conflicting statements and loopholes through which the Government might find an escape. But no man who brings to the subject the eye of an impartial historian can doubt that the pledge was originally given as an inducement to the pacification of the province, and that it has been renewed since in various forms. . . .

'The request for the fulfilment of that promise is not made by political agitators, but by a body of loyal proprietors who have done their utmost to strengthen the hands of the Government in all times of need, and who believe that fixity of tenure, more than any other measure, will enable them and their tenants to resist famine.'

share of the provincial revenues for imperial expenditure.*

It should be understood that this great increase in the military expenditure is not due to wars in India, for there have been no real wars within India during forty years, but to expeditions and defence works outside the limits of India. Conquests in the east as far as the frontiers of China and the dominions of France, conquests in the north in the wild and mountainous regions of Chitral, and the extension of the frontier line in the west into Afghanistan and Beluchistan, have been made and are maintained from the resources of India. These wild tracts, the Shan States of Burma in the east, and the mountains in the north and the west, can yield little revenue. The cost of maintaining troops, communications, and defence works in such tracts is enormous, and the old and peaceful Provinces of India are made to pay for these costly possessions outside the limits of India. A hope was held out to the people of India, and a

* 'The Madras Governor describes this system as alike demoralizing to the provinces, by rendering steady progress impossible, and to the Supreme Government of India, by enabling it to present a show of solvency without having recourse to extra taxation. The Lieutenant-Governor of Bengal, who rules one-third of the whole Indian population, tersely summarizes the actual results on each five years as "two years of screwing and saving and postponement of works, two years of resumed energy on a normal scale, and one year of dissipation of balances, in the fear that, if not spent, they will be annexed by the Supreme Government directly or indirectly at the next revision."'—*The Times*, June 7, 1897, Article on Indian Affairs.

pledge was given in the Queen's gracious Proclamation of 1858, that the cost of military expeditions outside the limits of India would not be charged to Indian revenues. Trans-frontier expeditions and conquests could not be undertaken out of Indian revenues under this pledge. The difficulty is got over by comprehending Burma and Chitral, Afghanistan and Beluchistan, under the name of 'India.' Is this not paltering with the people of India in a double sense, keeping the word of promise to our ear and breaking it to our hope?

A Royal Commission is now sitting to apportion expenditure as between England and India, and much valuable evidence has been given on the subject of the military expenditure of India. The evidence of Sir Henry Brackenbury, the military adviser to the Viceroy of India, is so important and so clear on the point we are now discussing, that we will quote it for our readers from an Indian journal. Sir Henry says:

'In the first place, I would say that the army in India is largely in excess of the requirements for the preservation of internal order in India. The strength of the army in India is calculated to allow of a powerful field army being placed on or beyond the Indian frontier, in addition to the obligatory garrisons required for keeping order in India. The necessity for maintaining in India the powerful field army in addition to the obligatory garrisons is caused by the approach of a great military power into a position which enables her directly to threaten Afghanistan, to which we are under treaty obligations, and indirectly to threaten the security of India itself. The foreign policy of India is directed entirely from England by Her Majesty's Government, and it is a part of British foreign policy generally—indeed, the object of British foreign policy, as I believe it to be—to secure Great Britain's rule over her empire. If we desired to maintain British rule in India only for India's sake, then I think it would be fair to make India pay to the uttermost farthing everything that it could be shown was due to Britain's rule over India. But I cannot but feel that England's interest—or Britain's interest—in keeping India under British rule is enormous. India affords employment to thousands of Britons, India employs millions of English capital, and Indian commerce has been of immense value to Great Britain. Therefore, it seems to me that India, being held by Great Britain not only for India's sake, but for Great Britain's sake, the latter should pay a share of the expenditure for this purpose. And in estimating what that share should be, I think that England should behave generously to India, because, in the first place, England is a rich country, and India is a poor country. It is not altogether a fair basis for a parallel between comparative richness and poorness, but it is one that may be worth bringing to notice, and that is the income-tax of India as compared with the income-tax of this country. In India you have an income-tax of 2½ per cent.—about sixpence in the pound—of which the product is less than a million sterling. In England one penny produces considerably over two millions. Indian taxation is chiefly derived from land revenue and the salt duties, and these fall ultimately on the poorer classes.'*

Sir Henry Brackenbury's opinion and arguments are sound, emphatic and clear, and we have no doubt Englishmen will be convinced of the justice and the growing necessity of contributing something to the cost of maintaining their great Asiatic empire, extending far beyond the natural limits of India, from which English commerce derives so much benefit. The shape which this contribution should take is a matter which deserves some consideration. It has been proposed that a fixed annual grant of about £1,000,000 should be made from the Imperial to the Indian Exchequer. Our own idea is, that such a fixed grant would be a loss to England, and would be no gain to India. The influences which make for increase in military expenditure are so strong in India, that the Imperial grant would soon be lost in the ever-widening gulf of frontier expenses, and the Indian tax-payer would not be benefited. We would propose, therefore, that Great Britain should pay some fixed proportion, however small it might be, of the entire military expenditure of India. This would give the tax-payers of Great Britain a control, which Indian tax-payers cannot ask for, over the entire Indian military expenditure. Sir Henry Brackenbury has said that if the question of the Indian frontier was done away with alto-

* *The Bengalee*, March 20, 1897.

gether, the Indian army might be reduced by 20,000 British troops and 50,000 Indian troops. This means about a third of the entire Indian army. Equitably and reasonably, therefore, England might be asked to pay a third share of the entire military expenditure of India. But if she pays even a fourth or a fifth of that expenditure, she would perceptibly relieve the Indian tax-payer. And the relief would come less from the contribution, directly made, than from the control over Indian military expenses which English tax-payers would then jealously exercise. From the nature of things, the Indian tax-payer cannot exercise that control. When the Viceroy and the Commander-in-Chief consider some new expenditure necessary, there is no authority in India that can ask the reason why. The Viceroy and the Commander-in-Chief are no doubt alive to the necessity of the utmost economy; but the most conscientious of spending departments in the world would work all the better for some efficient control.

We have dwelt so long on the subject of military expenditure, as it is probably the most prominent item of public expenditure in India. But the whole subject of Indian finances requires the most careful consideration; for the rate at which public expenditure under all heads has increased in India during the last thirty or forty years is alarming. The average annual revenue of Great Britain in 1851 to 1860 was £68,000,000; the average in 1881 to 1890 was £88,000,000; and the average during the last six years has been about £100,000,000. The revenue has thus slowly increased with the increase of population, and during a period of between forty and fifty years it has increased about 50 per cent. But what are the figures for India? The annual revenue in 1857—*i.e.*, after Dalhousie's last annexations, was Rx. 32,000,000; the annual revenue now, including railway receipts, is over Rx. 90,000,000; in other words, the revenue obtained from the country has nearly trebled in forty years.

Let us turn to the public debt. The National Debt of the United Kingdom was £826,000,000 in 1860. In 1896 it was £652,000,000, including the Suez Canal shares. In other words, the National Debt has been reduced by £174,000,000 in thirty-six years. In India the National Debt was £51,000,000 in 1857—*i.e.*, before the Mutiny. After the Mutiny it swelled to £97,000,000 in 1862; and in thirty years from that date it went up to nearly £200,000,000.* In other words, instead of being reduced, the National Debt was doubled within thirty years of internal peace in India, 1862 to 1892. It is scarcely a wise policy to add to the National Debt in times of peace. If the people of India had any voice in the management of their finances, they would have opposed such increase in the National Debt; they would have tried to reduce it, as it has been reduced in England.

* £107,000,000 in England, and Rx. 103,000,000 in India.

No doubt a large portion of the increase in the National Debt is due to the construction of railways and other public works in India. But a careful and prudent Government would have encouraged the construction of such works by private companies, without incurring debts, and without guaranteeing profits. English capital is undertaking vast public works all over Europe and in distant parts of the world, and surely English capital and enterprise would have opened out the high trade routes of India without the necessity of Government outlay. In exceptional cases, the Government may construct protective railways from its normal resources, but generally the construction of railways should be left to private enterprise. At present the Government of India has to remit about six millions a year to England for its railway obligations, and this is an important item of what are known as 'Home Charges.' A word or two about these charges are necessary.

The annual exports from India exceed the annual imports of merchandise and treasure by over £20,000,000. For this excess of exports over imports India receives no commercial equivalent; it is a steady drain on the resources of India. It comes to England partly as interest and profits on English capital invested in railways and other works in India, partly for army charges, and partly as the cost of the government of India from England. Roughly speaking, six millions are remitted to England for railway obligations, six millions for army charges, and some five or six millions more for stores, pensions, interest for ordinary debt, and other liabilities. Obligations contracted must be acquitted, and the serious drain on the resources of India must go on from year to year. But a prudent Government should endeavour to reduce its liabilities from year to year—its army charges and its railway obligations, the quantity of its imported stores, and the number of its European officials to whom pension has to be remitted out of India. It is by thus reducing liabilities in England and expenditure in India that it is possible to relieve our impoverished population.

These, then, are the remedies we have to propose for the poverty of the Indian masses. Indian problems are not the puzzles they are sometimes represented to be; Indian phenomena are not governed by other laws than those which govern the Universe. 'If a country,' said John Bright in 1853, 'be found possessing a most fertile soil, and capable of bearing every variety of production, and that notwithstanding the people are in a state of extreme destitution and suffering, the chances are there is some fundamental error in the government of that country.' The error was specified by Mr. Gladstone in 1893, when he said, 'the expenditure of India, and specially the military expenditure, is alarming.'

The remedies we have proposed are simple. A limit should be fixed to the State-demand from the produce of the soil, which is now virtually the sole means of the nation's subsistence after the decadence of the industries. And the expenditure of the Indian Government should be reduced, and England should contribute a fixed proportion of the military expenditure of India.

The third reform that we have to suggest is some healthy change in the system of administration. The administrative machinery has undergone some recent changes in towns and in seats of government; citizens in large towns are now allowed to manage their own concerns under some control; and a certain number of members are elected by the people to take their seats in Legislative Councils. But it may truly be said that in rural tracts the rude machinery of administration which was set up a hundred years ago, though modified and improved from time to time, has undergone no substantial and radical change. The One-Man Rule which was set up in every district by Warren Hastings remains radically the same after the lapse of over a century. The comprehensive and fantastically variegated powers with which the district officer was invested may have been a necessity in the early days of the British rule, but are unsuited to the present condition of India; they impede progress and make British administration more unpopular than it need be. The times call for a change, and it would be true statesmanship to introduce a change so greatly needed.

It would be difficult, within our limited space, to describe fully the powers which a district officer in India now exercises. We shall, therefore, specify only such of his powers as relate to the administration of justice. The district officer is the head of the police in his district; he directs investigation into heinous cases; he receives and peruses diaries sent up by investigating police-officers; he forms his opinion of a case from the perusal of these police diaries; and if the case appears to him to be true, he directs the case to be sent up for trial. When the case comes up, the district officer sends it to one of his own subordinate magistrates for trial, and he prosecutes the case through a subordinate police-officer. If the subordinate magistrate who tries the case is what is known in India as a second-class or a third-class magistrate, and if he convicts the prisoner, the prisoner's appeal lies to the district officer. We shall suppose that his appeal is rejected, and a sentence of hard labour passed on him is confirmed; the district officer is again the head of the local gaol, and sees how the prisoner is worked in gaol. To sum up, the district officer is the police-officer who directs the police investigation; he is the superior magistrate who has the prisoner tried by his own subordinate; he is the prosecutor who prosecutes the prisoner; he is the appellate court who hears the appeal if the prisoner is tried by a second or third class magistrate; and he is the head-gaoler who superintends the prisoner's work in the gaol.

The above is a brief account of the duties of a district officer in respect of criminal cases. It is scarcely possible to conceive that such duties of the police and the judge, of the prosecutor and the appellate court, are still kept in the same hands in any part of Her Majesty's dominions. The arrangement is needlessly making British administration unpopular in Indian districts; the educated people of India have loudly and frequently protested against it; and Englishmen, educated in the traditions of English law, have condemned the arrangement as opposed to all principles of equity and justice.

We have closely observed the work of Indian district officers for over a quarter of a century, and it is not our intention to say a word against district officers as a class. It is doubtful if there is any class of officers in any part of the British Empire who are charged with more severe and difficult duties than the Indian district officer. And we doubt very much if any class of officers in the world perform, on the whole, their difficult work more zealously, conscientiously, and ably. The charge which we bring is not against the men, but against the method—a method which was rudely shaped over a hundred years ago, and which has been allowed to remain radically unaltered in India, in spite of all judicial reforms which have taken place in England within this period.*

While some modification in the present method of district administration is thus urgently called for, it is also necessary to entrust the people in villages with

* We have shown elsewhere that the present defective arrangement in India can be modified without any material addition to expenditure. Into the details of such modification it is unnecessary to enter here.

some powers to deal with purely village concerns. Extreme centralization has been one of the mistakes of the existing system of rural administration in India. Disputes of a petty nature have to be brought up for decision in law-courts often twenty or thirty miles away from the scene of the dispute, and at such a distance the cases are often decided on the evidence of tutored witnesses. Civil causes and claims of money-lenders are also adjudicated in the law-courts with all the formalities of law. The authority of village elders and of village *Panchyets* is gone, and there is a rush of the agricultural population to law-courts, and to consequent impoverishment and ruin.

Village unions are now in the course of formation in different parts of India. It is possible to vest these bodies with some power to settle local disputes, and to adjudicate simple money-claims, and generally to manage the concerns of their villages. The subject is a large one and a difficult one, but if the principle be recognised, and an endeavour be made to carry it out, the experience of officers who have passed their lifetime in the work of Indian administration will surely suggest practicable methods of making the villagers of India partakers in the duty of administering their own concerns. The endeavour was made by Munro and Elphinstone early in this century, and it failed because village courts cannot exist side by side with higher tribunals empowered to adjudicate the same cases. This mistake may now be avoided, and with our experience of the last eighty years we may surely make the attempt again with greater chance of success.

The fourth and last reform which we venture to suggest is one which the educated classes in India have repeatedly urged, and urged with reason. A good government is a blessing to a country, but a good government conducted, as far as possible, by the people themselves is a higher blessing, because it elevates a nation. A benevolent administration such as India enjoys, is the first essential for the well-being of a country, but it is also essential that the people of the country should have a real and important share in conducting that administration. These are principles which have been recognised in modern times even by less civilized conquerors than the English, even by the Musulman conquerors of India and the Tartar conquerors of China. And these are principles which were acted upon, as far as was then possible, by early English rulers like Munro, Elphinstone, and Bentinck. But it must be admitted that within the last sixty years there has been no marked advance in this respect, commensurate with the marked progress of education in India. In the meantime the pledges given over sixty years ago have been repeated on the most solemn occasions, but the pledges remain virtually unredeemed.

At the renewal of the East India Company's Charter in 1833, it was declared in an Act of Parliament,

Act 3 and 4, William IV., c. 85, § 87: 'That no native of the said territories (India) nor any natural-born subject of her Majesty's resident therein shall, by reason only of his religion, place of birth, descent, colour, or any of them, be disabled from holding any place, office, or employment under the said Government.'

On the occasion when the Empire of India passed from the Company to the Crown, her Majesty the Queen declared in the famous Proclamation of 1858: 'And it is our further will that, so far as may be, our subjects, of whatever race or creed, be freely and impartially admitted to offices in our service, the duties of which they may be qualified by their education, ability and integrity, duly to discharge.'

And on the occasion when her Majesty the Queen assumed the august title of Empress of India, her Viceroy, Lord Lytton, declared at the Delhi Imperial Assemblage on January 1, 1877: 'You, the natives of India, whatever your race and whatever your creed, have a recognised claim to share largely with your English fellow subjects, according to your capacity for the task, in the administration of the country you inhabit. This claim is founded on the highest justice. It has been repeatedly affirmed by British and Indian statesmen, and by the legislation of the Imperial Parliament. It is recognised by the Government of India as binding on its honour, and consistent with all the aims of its policy.'

These are clear and emphatic pledges, given by England with the honest desire to redeem them, pledges which every schoolboy in India knows by heart, and desires to see redeemed. Yet how imperfectly these promises have been fulfilled will appear from the figures given below, compiled from the India List of the present year (1897), and showing the higher appointments in the principal civil departments, held by Europeans and Indians respectively, in the five populous and advanced Provinces of India:

Nature of Appointments.	Bengal.		North-West.		Punjab.		Madras.		Bombay.	
	Europeans.	Indians.	Europeans.	Indians.	Europeans.	Indians.	Europeans.	Indians.	Europeans.	Indians.
Judges of High Courts and Chief Courts	9	3	5	1	3	2	5	1	4	2
District and Sessions and Divisional Judges ...	26	3	24	2	15	2	21	0	15	1
Members of Board and Commissioners...	11	0	10	0	6	0	4	0	3	0
District Magistrates and Collectors and Deputy Commissioners...	40	5	49	0	38	2	22	0	23	0
Chief Engineers, Superintending Engineers and Executive Engineers, including Irrigation Branch	34	1	56	2	60	4	42	2	40	9
Higher Education Officers...	27	4	12	0	8	2	22	2	20	7
Higher Police Officers ...	59	2	49	1	55	0	33	0	28	0
Civil Medical Officers ...	57	8	47	1	31	1	25	2	41	4
Special Gaol Officers ...	14	0	7	0	4	0	7	0	4	0
Forest Officers	13	0	19	0	10	0	27	2	26	1

If the figures given above be correct, and they have been compiled from the names given in the India List for the current year, then it will appear that out of over a hundred district and divisional judges in the five advanced Provinces of India, only 8 are Indians; that out of nearly two hundred district officers, only 7 are Indians; that there are 16 Indian doctors of the higher rank out of over two hundred; that there are 3 Indian higher police officers out of over two hundred; and the number of Indian engineers is only 18 out of over two hundred. The proportion of Indian officers in the higher grades of the Postal, the Telegraph, and the Opium Departments is still smaller; and the proportion of Indian officers in the less advanced Provinces is, of course, very much smaller. It is said that a sudden change in the *personnel* of the different services is undesirable, and that it is necessary to have a fair proportion of Englishmen in all the civil departments of the Indian Service. Making every allowance for these alleged reasons, it is still impossible for any unbiassed judge to run his eye over the figures given, and to say that an honest endeavour has been made within the last sixty years to give to the people of India a fair share of the higher appointments.

The question is not about the salary of a few hundred or a few thousand appointments being drawn by Englishmen or by Indians; the question is, if Indians of education, ability, and integrity should still be virtually excluded from a real share in directing the civil administration of their own country. The question was decided over sixty years ago by Lord William Bentinck in respect of the subordinate judicial and executive services; and it remains for some equally large-hearted statesman of the present day to settle it in reference to the higher services. Such a settlement of the question is inevitable; England desires, and India expects, that the pledges which England has given to the people of India shall be honourably redeemed.

Closely connected with this question is the question of an extension in the principle of representation: not representation in the sense in which it is understood in England, but representation in the sense in which it has been introduced in India, and has worked well. The elective principle was introduced in a limited way in district and municipal committees by Lord Ripon during his wise and beneficent administration of India, and, under the more recent India Councils Act of 1892, elected members are allowed to take their seat in Legislative Councils. The measures which were introduced, almost experimentally, have worked well, and the local knowledge possessed and the intelligent interest evinced by elected members, have greatly contributed to good administration. Educated Indians have asked that the elective principle may now be extended, and that elected members be allowed to take a larger share in the administration of the country. The request is reasonable and just, and, judging from our experience of recent years, a concession in this direction is likely to be beneficial.

There is no abler or more devoted body of public

servants in the world than the English administrators who have undertaken the government of India; but it is no reflection against these alien rulers to state that frequent and serious mistakes might be avoided, and more complete success in civil administration might be secured, if they availed themselves, to a greater extent than they have yet done, of the opinion, the advice, and the co-operation of the enlightened leaders of the people. In the highest centres of the Indian Government, in the Council of the Secretary of State, in the Executive Council of the Viceroy, in the Secretariats and Executive Councils of the Provincial Governments, Indian opinion is unrepresented. And in the Imperial Parliament which controls the administration of India, the people of India have no representative, and the proposal made some time ago of sending up one or two members from each Indian Province has been heard of no more. No great and civilized country like India is ruled in the present day under a form of government in which the people are so utterly unrepresented.

The time is now come when, in the face of the grave difficulties which surround us, and in which Indian leaders are peculiarly fitted to advise and to help, the English rulers of India may consider it desirable to associate themselves more largely with those men whom the people of the country may elect to give expression to their feelings, their wishes, and their aspirations.

India has outgrown the form of administration which was framed on the assumption of the government by the Crown, forty years ago, and after the suppression of a great rebellion. Education has spread in the country within these forty years; millions of Indians have been educated in English and vernacular schools in India; thousands of them have travelled in Europe and completed their education in England. Steam and telegraph have brought the people of India closer to England; loyal and influential political bodies have taught them the methods of constitutional agitation; and the very spread of the idea of imperial federation has inspired them with the hope that India, though only a dependency, has deserved, and will receive, some measure of self-government, along with the other parts of England's world-wide empire.

A feeling of unrest is perceptible in India, not of unrest under the British rule, but of unrest under a form of government framed forty years ago, and which no longer suits the circumstances of the present day. There is danger in exaggerating this feeling, but it were folly to close our eyes to it altogether. And the secret of this feeling of unrest is this, that educated Indian opinion and sentiment and ambition are struggling against that cast-iron form of administration which has not expanded with the times. Indian opinion seeks to be heard, and is not heard; Indian feeling seeks to be represented, and is not represented. It is easy to condemn this desire as discontent, or even disloyalty, but Englishmen must know that it is neither one nor the other. It is a natural feeling produced by antiquated methods of government after the country has outgrown those methods. It is a feeling which Englishmen would have felt to-day, if the old system of representation had not been reformed by the Acts of 1832, 1867, and 1884.

England now stands at the parting of the ways in regard to Indian administration. She can continue to rule India regardless of the wishes of the people, and according to the method constructed forty years ago. She can continue to keep the door closed against any real representation of Indian opinion and Indian feeling in the government of the country. She can refuse to allow to the people of the country a real and legitimate share in conducting and directing the administration. She can turn a deaf ear to the growing demand to make the administration more liberal, more in touch with the people, more in consonance with the progress of the times. And she can decline the counsels and the co-operation of the people in her endeavours to ameliorate their condition, to readjust finances, and to face scarcities and famines. England has the power to proceed on these lines if she thinks it a wise course.

There is yet a second course which England can adopt. Without yielding in the slightest degree her hold over India, she may yet admit the children of the soil into a larger share of administrative power. Strong in maintaining order among the various races and nationalities of India, she may yet seek to minimize the chances of disorder and the causes of discontent by allowing some system of representation to those races. Determined to hold the balance evenly among the different Indian communities, and to rule with firmness as well as with justice, she may still invite the natural leaders of those communities to partake more largely in the work of administration, and to enlighten the Government with their views and opinions on questions affecting their welfare. And maintaining her strong rule over the great continent peopled by nearly three hundred millions of men, she may yet allow that vast population some carefully guarded system of representation, some method of being consulted and heard in the management of their own concerns.

The second course would strengthen, not weaken, the power of England in India. The one weak point in English administration in India is that want of sympathy which Elphinstone deplored sixty years ago, that want of touch with the people which keeps the Government ignorant of their real wants and feelings, that want of intimate local knowledge which leads even a wise administration into blunders and mistakes which sometimes result in serious consequences. It is possible to remove this want by inviting the representatives of the people themselves to co-operate more largely in the work of administration, and it is possible to enlist the natural ambition of leading Indians, the growing aspirations of educated Indians, and the willing advocacy of the press itself in the cause of British administration, instead of estranging them by an exclusive policy. An exclusive policy is, under the present circumstances, both weakness and folly; a policy of recognising the just influences and aspirations of the people is a policy of strength as well as of wisdom. The former policy makes the British administration liable to errors and mistakes, and makes the entire public opinion of the country keen and eager to criticize those mistakes. The latter policy would lessen the chances of mistakes, and would enlist the public opinion of India in the work of rectifying those mistakes. The former policy needlessly creates difficulties by excluding the people's co-operation and estranging their public opinion; the latter policy would smooth the work of administration by throwing it partly on the people themselves, and would enlist Indian public opinion in the cause of Indian administration. The former is a difficult and a thankless task; the latter would be an easy and a grateful task.

The power of England in India is strong, and every official, who has worked in India, knows that England needs be immensely strong amidst the vast and various populations of India. But they are foolish advisers who say that England's strength lies in an exclusive policy, in a policy of suspicion and of distrust. They mislead England who urge that her strength lies in debarring the people of India from the higher spheres of administration, and in estranging public opinion and the press. And they create difficulties in the work of administration who argue that England's strength lies in repressing the natural ambition and aspirations of the people. As we have said before, this is the one weak point in the present administration of India: the administration is not in touch with the people, does not represent the wishes and feelings of the people, does not enlist the co-operation and the sympathy of the people. It is the one weak point of British rule in India that it is not sufficiently cognizant of the feelings of the people, that it does not sufficiently accept the co-operation of the natural leaders and representatives of the people, and that it is conducted by a handful of alien rulers, who, however able and well disposed, do not know the people, cannot mix with the people, and are less in touch with the people to-day than English administrators were in the time of Munro and Elphinstone. This is the one cause to which may be traced many of the mistakes in administration described in this chapter.

The time is come when an endeavour may be made to remedy this defect. The time is come when in the midst of the difficulties of the present administration, in the midst of poverty and famine, of financial distress, and of general unrest, some methods of conciliation may be adopted, and a larger share of confidence and of work may be reposed on the people. The time is come when the rulers of India may bestow on the people of India a carefully-guarded system of representation, and a larger share in civil and military administration. We read in ancient history that the

Roman conquerors of Gaul admitted the chiefs of the conquered nations to seats in the Roman Senate House and to commands in the imperial army. The modern nation whose proud boast it is to have inherited the imperial power and the imperial instincts of ancient Rome cannot rule a greater and more civilized empire in a different spirit—in a spirit of jealousy, distrust, and exclusiveness. And if we have read the history of the last hundred years aright, we find in it not only the story of steady constitutional progress in the past, but the promise of constitutional progress in the future. And we found on it the hope that with the advancement of England in the future, as an imperial power in the world, the people of India shall obtain some share, such as it may be considered feasible and wise to concede, of those representative institutions and that system of self-government which are the birthright of the nations united to-day in paying a common homage to the Queen of England.

APPENDIX

INDIAN EXPENDITURE IN 1887 AND 1897.

The Indian Budget for the current year has been published in England after the preceding pages were written, and we take the liberty of placing before our readers in this Appendix a few figures showing the alarming increase in taxation and expenditure in India in recent years. During the decade 1887-1897 there has been in the British Isles an accumulated net remission of taxation of £21,000,000,* and during this decade there has been no remission of taxation in India (except a modification of cotton duties, made in the interests of Lancashire), but there has been an accumulated imposition of new taxation amounting in the aggregate to Rx. 29,000,000. This is the essential difference between the financial policy of England and the financial policy of India in times of uninterrupted peace. The strain of taxation is relaxed in England in times of peace; the strain of taxation goes on ever increasing in India.

Let us now turn to figures. Excluding revenue, which is collected but refunded, and excluding railway receipts,

* The figures in this Appendix are taken from a Special Article in the *Daily Chronicle* of August 5, 1897.

the revenues of India have increased thus in the last ten years:

[Rx. = nominally £1.]

	1887-1888 (Accounts). Rx.		1897-1898 (Budget). Rx.
I. LAND REVENUE:			
i. Land	23,141,300	...	25,601,800
ii. Forest	1,121,700	...	1,753,000
Total ...	24,263,000		27,354,800
II. TRIBUTES	743,600	...	901,600
III. OPIUM	6,089,100	...	3,156,200
IV. TAXATION:			
i. Salt	6,636,200	...	8,698,800
ii. Stamps	3,832,000	...	4,782,600
iii. Excise	4,501,000	...	5,653,800
iv. Provincial rates ...	3,027,400	...	3,616,000
v. Customs	1,316,800	...	4,375,900
vi. Assessed taxes. ...	1,411,500	...	1,836,800
vii. Registration	310,200	...	439,700
Total ...	21,035,100		29,403,600
V. MISCELLANEOUS	986,700	...	366,800
TOTAL REVENUE	53,117,500	...	61,183,000

It will be seen from the above figures that the loss in Opium Revenue is made up by the increase in Land Revenue, and that Rx. 8,000,000 more are raised by Taxation in the current year than what was raised ten years ago. It is estimated that of this increase, something above Rx. 3,000,000 represents the natural increment in the revenues due to growth in population, etc. The balance of Rx. 5,000,000 means an increase in the incidence of taxation during a period of profound peace in India. It is an increase which should be unnecessary in times of peace, and is both inexpedient and unjust.

Let us examine the figures once more. The total increase in revenue in these ten years is over Rx. 8,000,000. Rx. 5,000,000 out of this increase are contributed by the State demand on land and by tax on salt. The two articles on which the poorest of the poor depend for their subsistence in India, viz., the produce from land and salt, contribute the largest increase in the revenues during the past decade. This, again, is both inexpedient and unjust.

Let us now turn to the net expenditure for 1887-88 and 1897-98. The figures are set forth below.

[Rx. = nominally £1.]

	1887-1888 (Accounts). Rx.		1897-1898 (Budget). Rx.
I. COLLECTION OF REVENUE :			
i. Land	3,486,700	...	4,166,700
ii. Forest	719,800	...	1,076,100
iii. Taxes	1,114,100	...	1,474,900
iv. Assignments	1,467,300	...	1,553,300
Total ...	6,787,900		8,271,000
II. DEBT SERVICES... ...	4,695,200	...	2,708,700
III. CIVIL SERVICES :			
i. Departments... ...	11,410,600	...	13,778,600
ii. Miscellaneous.. ...	3,974,200	...	5,242,400
iii. Buildings and roads	3,667,100	...	3,919,300
Total ...	19,061,900		22,940,300

	[Rx. = nominally £1.] 1887-1888 (Accounts). Rx.		1897-1898 (Budget). Rx.
IV. MILITARY SERVICES:			
i. Army	19,357,100	...	23,314,200
ii. Military Works ...	1,191,700	...	1,181,200
iii. Special Defence ...	456,000	...	19,400
Total ...	21,004,800		24,514,800
V. COMMERCIAL SERVICES:			
Net cost of Post Office, Railways, Irrigation	3,053,500	...	2,728,700
VI. RAILWAY CONSTRUCTION	81,000	...	7,300
VII. FAMINE RELIEF AND INSURANCE ...	91,400	...	3,666,200
TOTAL EXPENDITURE ...	54,775,700		64,837,000

The first thing which strikes one in examining these figures is the alarming increase in expenditure, within a period of ten years of profound peace. In these ten years the revenues have increased by Rx. 8,000,000, while the expenditure has increased by Rx. 10,000,000. The largest increases are in Famine Relief and Insurance, in the Civil Services, and in the Military Services, there being an increase of between Rx. 3,000,000 and Rx. 4,000,000 under each of these heads. One or two remarks under each of these heads will suffice.

The increase under the head of Famine Relief and Insurance is consequent on the poverty of the people and of recurring famines. The special expenditure under this head cannot be altogether saved until the general condition of the people has improved. Till then the impoverished people must be taxed in order to be saved from death.

The Civil Services show an increase of nearly Rx. 4,000,000, a million out of which may be put down to Exchange. It is a notorious fact that the price of food has risen in India fifty per cent. or more within these forty years; but natives of India, employed in Government offices as clerks or ministerial officers on a humble pay of about a shilling a day, have been allowed no compensation and no increase of pay for their increased cost of living. But European officers, who are supposed to make remittances to Europe to their families or friends, or for the purpose of saving, are allowed a special compensation from the Indian Exchequer because the rupee has gone down in value in comparison with gold. And in the higher Indian services, recruited in England, a distinction in remuneration is made virtually on the ground of colour and race; the European is allowed an Exchange compensation, and the Indian who has entered the same service by the same examination in London is allowed none. To such acts of unfairness and petty self-seeking the most conscientious governments will sometimes descend when the people governed are allowed no voice and no influence in the administration of their country.

Lastly, the Military Services show an increase of over Rx. 3,000,000. The military expenditure in 1887 was heavy enough, because the hunt for a 'scientific frontier' had been made by Disraeli and Lord Lytton years before, and an extended frontier had already increased the military expenditure of India. The further increase within the last ten years shows the steady growth in the costliness of the Indian army which neither the poverty of the people nor famines can retard for a moment. The military department, we have said elsewhere, is under no effective control; the people of India have no voice in its arrangements; and the people of England do not trouble themselves about it so long as they do not pay. And so it comes to pass that *nearly one half of the net revenues of India is spent on the military services.* For the total budgeted revenue of the current year is Rx. 61,000,000, and the cost of collecting this revenue is Rx. 8,000,000. The net revenue, therefore, is Rx. 53,000,000, and Rx. 24,500,000 out of this is spent on the military services.

India cannot be prosperous and contented until her military expenditure is revised and reduced. And in justice and in equity, England should bear a portion of the cost of that army which she maintains in India in furtherance of her imperial policy, and in defence of her Eastern Empire from which she benefits so largely in her trade and in the profitable employment of her capital. A contribution of a fixed proportion of the Indian military expenditure from the English exchequer would be an act of simple justice which England owes to India, would secure an effective control over that expenditure, and would be a real relief to the people of India, suffering from chronic poverty, increasing taxation, and recurring famines.

THE END.